WOMEN AND EMPOWERMENT

WOMEN AND EMPOWERMENT

JAYA KOTHAI PILLAI

GYAN PUBLISHING HOUSE
NEW DELHI-110 002

Women and Empowerment

ISBN: 81-212-0512-3

Reprinted in 2011 in India by
Gyan Publishing House
23, Main Ansari Road, Daryaganj,
New Delhi - 110002
Phone : 23282060, 23261060
Fax : (011) 23285914
E-mail : books@gyanbooks.com
Website: gyanbooks.com

Printed at: G. Print Process, Delhi

PREFACE

Empowerment is an active, multi dimensional process which enables women to realise their full identity and powers in all spheres of life. Power is not a commodity to be transacted; nor can it be given away as alms. "Power has to be acquired and once acquired, it needs to be exercised, sustained and preserved." Women have to empower themselves. This means that they have to understand the causes of the existing inequality of women in all sectors—economic, social, political, legal and educational—and take the initiative to change their status.

The book is in two Sections, the first dealing with empowerment of women in general and the second section, empowerment of women professionals.

The papers in Chaper 1, "The Setting" analyses the existing status of the female child, the legal rights of women, the views of Gandhi and Nehru on Women's rights and traces the social and economic development of women since independence with suggestions for liberation of women in the Indian context.

The papers in chapter 2 portray the profiles of some rural women—the agricultural labourers and head loaders, examines the possible adverse effects of the New Economic policy on the development of poor women and shows how the involvement and integration of rural women in development are vital for economic and social success of the country.

Chapter 3 has papers on the main theme, the strategies of empowerment, the new roles for education, the importance of the academic discipline of women's studies as a powerful tool to the cause of women's liberation and strategies for advancement of women into upper management positions.

In Section II, research studies done on four categories of women professionals—women physicians, women engineers, women lawyers and women managers—have been reviewed, research findings of current and past researches have been scanned and the 'agreed upon' findings have been highlighted.

This exhaustive review was possible only because of the library privileges offered while the author was a visiting scholar to Henry Murray Research Center of Radelitte College, Cambridge, Massachusetts, USA. The author is very grateful to the President; Radelitte College for offering her a visiting scholar appointment.

The last paper contains the advice given by some successful women professionals to young ambitious women who are interested in advancing in their careers.

These papers have been put together with the hope that it would be useful to all those concerned with the issues of women's development and advancement.

Madras

J. K. Pillai

CONTENT

Section I

Section II

SECTION-I

1

THE SETTING

The Female Child in India

Women's Rights and Social Change

Women and Consumer Protection Rights

Gandhi and Nehru on Women's Rights

Social and Economic Development of Women in the last few decades

Liberation of Women in the Indian Context

THE FEMALE CHILD IN INDIA

The United Nations declaration on the Rights of the Child (1959) maintains that "mankind owes to the child the best it can give". The U.N. convention of 1989, the most exhaustive international expression of children's rights starts with the statement "Children, because of their vulnerability, need special care and protection". The human rights of the child includes civil, political, economic, social and cultura rights. The civil rights under the convention include the right to a name and nationality, protection from torture and maltreatment. The economic rights include the right to benefit from social security, the right to a standard of living, and right for protection from exploitation at work. The social rights include the right to highlight attainable standard of health and access to medical services, the right to special care for handicapped children, protection from abduction and social exploitation and regulation of adoption. Cultural rights include the child's right to develop fully through education.

The Child in India

In the Indian context, let us examine how far the rights of the child are protected. Even the most fundamental right— the right to survive is not discharged properly. Approximately 4.2 million children die in India mostly from preventable diseases. The average infant mortality rate in the first year of birth is 10% and in the slum areas it is 12.4%. Children dying because of malnutrition before the age of 5 years is about 40%.

India ranks 30th among countries with 152 deaths per 1000 live births. The most important reason for this high death rate of children is that the majority of Indian children are vulnerable and deprived of medical and rehabilitation facilities.The energy intake of lower income family children is found to be 30% below the recommended levels. Nearly 85% of Indian children suffer from varying degrees of malnutrition. About 63% of children below 3 years and 45% between 3 and 5 years suffer from iron deficiency and anaemia. Thousands of children go blind every year by the deficiency of vitamin A. Only 15% of the population has access to hospitals.

According to a UNICEF survey report of 1984, in India, there were 2.5 lakhs blind, 2.5 lakhs deaf and 5 lakhs orthopedically handicapped children. Neither the Government nor the voluntary agencies have been able to even touch the fringe of this problem of growing incidence of childhood disabilities.

The number of destitute children is rapidly increasing with the collapse of the traditional family and social structures. Welfare services for such children is almost negligible. A rough estimate is that the total number of orphan children would be around 30 million.

Among the World's working children, Indian Children constitute the largest number, anywhere around 16 to 17 million. These children work from 6-12 hours a day and they are employed in agriculture, industry and domestic work.

When we consider education, we find that illiteracy, ignorance and low status of women have direct bearing on children, their health and education. Areas where there is low female literacy, are also characterised by under-development, low employment, low per capita income, low nutritional level with heavy concentration of scheduled communities and landless agricultural workers. Low female literacy is highly correlated to high fertility rates, high population growth rate, and high infant and child mortality rate. There is a high association of female literacy with female age at marriage, life expectancy, participation in modern sectors of economy and female enrolment in schools.

Even after four decades of our independence, all children of 6-14 age group are not in schools. Only 56.3% of the boys and 30.6% of the girls of the relevant age specific population have been enrolled. Nearly 1/5th of the total habitations have no schools of their own. And even where schools exist, 40% have no pucca building, 39.72% have no black boards, 59.50 have no drinking water and 35% of the schools are single teacher schools.

Primary education has not improved qualitatively in most of the rural and backward areas. The subjects taught are not related to the environment of children; the methods of teaching are outmoded, rigid, and uninteresting; work based or activity based education has not been implemented. All these have led to dropping out of the children from the schools. Of 100 children enrolled in class I only 23 reach class VIII, attaining the desired level of literacy.

The Female Child

Girl children today are targets of attack even before they are born. Even among the educated, urban, well-to-do people, advanced medical technology such as amniocentesis and super sonography are used and if the foetus is found to be female, abortion is induced. In a sample study, 7999 of 8000 foetuses aborted were female. According to a Times of India report in June 1982, in the four years after the introduction of sex detection tests in our country between 1978-82, 78000 female foetuses were aborted. Even before the girl child is born, parents view her as a liability. This attitude is rooted in a complex set of social, cultural and historical factors. The dowry system, economic dependence of women and social customs and traditions are the main causes of the neglect of the girl child and discrimination against her.

As the girl child is viewed as an economic burden and social responsibility, she is unwanted and her arrival is not considered as a joy and discrimination begins immediately after birth, with respect to feeding practices, health and medical care. Various reports on the duration of breast feeding indicate preference for longer feeding for boys; the interval between births is shorter after the birth of a girl than after the birth of a boy, indicating a shorter period of breast feeding for the female child (Helder and Bhattacharya 1969).

Among some groups, it is reported that the ceremony of annaprashna, i.e, giving the first solid food, is earlier for girls than for boys, indicating a shorter duration of exclusive breast feeding.

It has been brought out by Miller in his book "The Endangered Sex" (1981) and confirmed by the Operation Research group of Baroda (1986) that there was a definite preference favouring boys with regards to eggs, milk and butter.

There is considerable evidence of higher morbidity among girls. Dandekar, in his survey of rural communities found that the percentage of children getting no medical treatment was higher in females. During an observation period of one week at a primary health centre, Khan observed that 43 boys attended the centre as compared to 15 girls and discrimination against girls increased with their number in the family. Child Mortality data shows a bias against females. Taking the first five years as a whole, the death rate of female children was 74 per 1000 while the death rate of male children was 50 per 1000. Girls less than 2 years old had substantially smaller chances of survival than boys of the same age. A comparative study of child mortality notes that in the overall pattern, there was poorer child care with respect to female children in the northern states related to southern states but there is a recent report from Tamil Nadu about female infanticide in the district of Madurai.

It is also found that there is no linkage between the prosperity of a family and the status of the girl child. In Punjab and Haryana, for instance, the mortality of the girl children is striking despite the high per capita income. Higher mortality rate among girl children leads to an adverse sex ratio. It is alarming to find that the sex ratio has further declined from 933 in 1981 to 929 in 1991 per 1000 males. We need to organise mass campaign to raise social consciousness in favour of the girl child among all sections of people.

In the rural areas, about 70% of the non-starters i.e. those who have never been to schools are girls. As mothers took on the role of the girl as a second mother to took after the younger siblings and shoulder the responsibility of household work, in charge of fetching water, fuel, fodder, cleaning and cooking, the girl child gets handicapped and conditioned by the attitude of the mother and the family and the traditional sex role, and going to school becomes secondary. The economic value of the girl child, to the family and to the society is never recognised. According to a U.N. report, on an average, a girl in the third world countries, works for 9 hours a day for 315 days in a year in the home and in the fields, as unpaid labour and by the time she ceases to be a child, she renders economic help worth Rs. 39600 at minimum wages surviving on substandard food and struggling against prejudice and discrimination.

When the father or brother is a drunkard, the girl child, in many cases, is physically assaulted, insulted and abused. These traumative experiences leave a lasting impression on the girl child. There are quite a few instances of sexual abuse of the girl child, of her being seduced and led into prostitution, of unwanted pregnancies and sexually transmitted diseases. The incidences of child marriage continues in spite of the legal prohibition. This leads to early pregnancy, and puts pressure on the child to play adult roles.

There are any amount of social prejudices against the girl child. A proverb goes like this "Bringing up a daughter is like watering a plant in the neighbour's gardern". In the census data of a village in U.P, it was found that the village women did not bother to include girls in the number of children. The reason stated was that girls have only temporary membership in the parental home, they are considered as guests in their native village and that they would be sent away in marriage, bonded to some other village as soon as the parents can arrange. It was also considered unnecessary to spend money on girls—on their health or education. The female child, in Indian culture, is expected to cultivate the qualities of inferiority, subservience and domesticity which place severe limitations on her growth and development.

During the years 1971-81, girl child labour increased four times as that of boys. Thus the initial investment on the girl is well below the minimum prescribed in any charter of Human Rights. The female child population in India is around 160 million today and is the most vulnerable group.

The greatest single factor which can improve the status of the girl child is education—education of the girls, their parents, and the society in general.

There is lower enrolment of girls in schools and higher drop-out rate from the schools. According to the latest statistics, two out of every ten girls in the age group 6-11 are still not enrolled in schools. The incidences of drop out and stagnation amongst girls is nearly twice that of boys. The Government have set up anganwadis, balwadis etc. to look after the younger siblings of the school going girls. The nutritious noon meal scheme with all the package benefits of free education, free books, free uniforms etc. have also contributed to some extent to the regular attendance and retention of children in the schools in Tamil Nadu. These should be strengthened.

Nutrition and health care should be adequately taught in schools. Adolescent girls should be trained in fertility awareness education so that they have the knowledge and skills to prevent molestation and rape. Girls should be trained in vocational skills and should be educated with a view to achieving ultimate economic independence.

The electronic media should launch a campaign of education inputs to depict the girl child in a positive light. This would help in changing the society's attitude towards girls and their roles.

The print media should give enough space or priority to reports on health and nutrition. Discriminatory advertising should stop both in the print and electronic media.

In short, girls should be helped to grow up to be human beings.

It is high time we started thinking of the importance of nutrition and health status of women as individuals and in terms of human resource development and not only in terms of her maternal status.

References

Challenge of Education: National Policy on Education - Ministry of Human Resource Development, Govt. of India, 1986.

National Perspective Plan for Women 1988-2000 A.D.- Ministry of State for Youth Affairs, Sports and Women and Child, Ministry of Human Resource Development, Government of India, 1988.

Towards Equality - Report of the committee on status of women in India 1974.

WOMEN'S RIGHTS AND SOCIAL CHANGE

Introduction

The concept that "Woman is as much a human being as man and thus entitled to the same freedom, rights and responsibilities" is yet to find universal acceptance in spite of the unequivocal assertion that women have complete and equal rights with men in every respect by the International Bill of Human Rights. This has been reiterated right from 1945, in the Charter of the United Nations and then in the convention on elimination of all forms of discrimination against women in 1967 and the Nairobi Declaration in 1979.

The Constitution of India has guaranteed equality, liberty and dignity to the women of India. The preamble promises to secure to all its citizens justice—economic, social and political, liberty of thought, expression, belief, faith and worship, equality of status and opportunity and to promote among them all, fraternity as suring the dignity of the individual and the unity of the nation.

The fundamental rights, the directive principles and the fundamental duties give equal status to women and also provide special protection. Improvement in the status of women was a pledge made by the Constitution and admitted by the Government as one of the major tasks. Some laws attempting to embody the principles underlying the Constitution have been passed through the legislature. Modern society relies heavily on law to bring about social changes.

Historical Perspective

Some reforms in law and legal customs had been pushed through by the British and Indian social reformers like Raja Ram Mohan Roy during the 19th Century itself. If it was an accepted social norm, legislature legitimacy became significant, for example abolition of 'Sati'. But female infanticide, child marriage, enforced widowhood etc. prevailed inspite of legislation like Hindu Widow Re-marriage Act of 1856, Child Marriage Restraint Act of 1929 and Hindu Women's Right to Property Act of 1929 and 1937. Due to diversities in personal laws among the major religions and their interpretations, disparity of status between men and women and discrimination among women themselves continued.

In Article 14, the Constitution guarantees every person equality and equal protection, article 15 prohibits discrimination on grounds of religion, race, caste, sex, place of birth etc. Article 16(2) proclaims that there should be no discrimination on grounds of sex in employment; Article 23 is against exploitation; Article 39 (d) promises equal work, Article 42 recommends just and humane conditions of work and maternity relief; but Article 25, which allows freedom of religion takes precedence over other civil laws especially in the two areas of marriage and the family structure and ownership of property.

Political Equality

There are rights conferred on women by the Constitution and rights conferred on them legally; political equality is granted to women under the Indian Constitution, guaranteed through instrument of adult franchise and by Article 15 which prohibits discrimination on grounds of sex. But the Constitution as sanction is enjoyed only to a limited extent by women in reality. More and more women are now actively participating in the political process but only a few women hold elected positions, fewer still are so placed as to be able to influence in political thinking. There is greater awareness among women of the power that the right of franchise has given to them, but the extent of awareness varies significantly between different groups and different religions. The level of literacy and urbanisation have an impact on the awareness, but the political parties have generally been indifferent towards women and treating them more as appendices to men.

Legislature Enacted After Independence

Since Independence, quite a few laws have been passed and some have been amended so as to provide equitable share to women in property as well as to eradicate some of the injustices meted out to women. The Hindu Marriage Act of 1955 confers on women the rights for judicial separation, restitution of conjugal rights and divorce by mutual consent. The Hindu Succession Act of 1956 abolished the age-old Dayabhaga system and included the wife and mother in Class I heirs, sharing equally the properties of the deceased along with the son and daughter. By the Hindu Adoption and Maintenance Act of 1956, Hindu women get the status of Coparcener and the rights of survivorship. According to this Act, even unmarried girls above 18 can adopt anybody—boy or girl. The Dowry Prohibition Act of 1961 prohibited giving or taking of property or valuable security as consideration for marriage. The Immoral Traffic Prevention Act of 1956, Medical Termination of Pregnancy Act of 1971 and the Indecent Representation of Women Prevention Act of 1986 try to safeguard the modesty, reputation and chastity of women folk. The Sati Prevention Act of 1987 is a central law that seeks not only to prevent and punish the Commission of the Act itself, but also to make an offence any glorfication of the Act of Sati. Under the Maternity Benefit Act, benefits such as six weeks paid leave at the time of delivery, bonus or post natal care etc. accrued to women. Equal Remuneration Act of 1976 and 1987 ensured equal pay for equal work and to take care of any discrimination on grounds of gender during employment. Thus, by stages steps have been taken by piecemeal legislation to raise the status of women, socially, economically and politically.

The two land-marks in the legal history of Women's struggle for equal rights are the cases of C.B. Muthamma and that of airhostesses. C.B. Muthamma was the first foreign Service Officer who challenged the service rule which debarred foreign service women from marrying without permission when no such requirement was there for males. The airhostesses challenged the rule which terminated their services if they got married within four years of recruitment or pregnancy and termination of service at 35 years of age. The court ruled that their services should extend to 45 years but could not marry within four years of recruitment.

Laws Repugnant to the Constitution

There are laws repugnant to the Constitution for e.g.

(1) Personal and family law discriminate not only between men and women but between women and women as well.

(2) Army Act, Navy Act, Air Force Act and Service rules discriminate against women.

(3) A woman in India is not the natural guardian of her children.

(4) As there is no community of property, a woman is not entitled to an equal share in the property of the husband.

(5) There is no money value to the work of the women in the home.

(6) A Hindu woman is not entitled by birth to a share in the joint family property nor can she ask for partition of the property.

(7) A Muslim woman is discriminated against in matters of marriage, divorce, maintenance and inheritance.

  (a) Polygamy is permitted (not Polyandry).

  (b) By pronouncing "Talak" three times a wife can be divorced.

  (c) A male child is entitled to a share of two females.

(8) A Parsi woman, if she marries out of the community she ceases to be a Parsi and a Parsi daughter is discriminated against in matters of inheritance.

Lacunae and Loopholes

There are many lacunae in laws and many loopholes in the enforcement of laws.

There is no law to combat dowry crimes, there is no legal bar against a man marrying the next day after burning his wife.

The law of maintenance is unjust, cumbersome, duplicate and dilatory; a Hindu woman is entitled to maintenance under the Act of 1955 & 1956, but she has to move the court for which she might not have the money.

Failure of the law enforcing agencies, especially the police, is another reason for the ineffectiveness of the laws. As soon as laws are passed, the rules and regulations should also be framed and an infrastructure and implementation machinery must form part of the Statutes. Awareness programmes should be planned and funds made available for the programme; merely, the law alone cannot bring about social revolution; adequate infrastructure also should be provided; family courts, special boards for dowry complaints, rape cases etc. are necessary.

Amendments to existing laws such as Hindu Marriage Act, Child Marriage Restraint Act, Equal Remuneration Act etc. were passed due to pressures from informed and articulate sections of the people. But reporting is delayed or distorted. Police force is not equipped to deal with crimes both professionally and psychologically. The long established social and cultural traditions of Indian life influence the ignorant policemen and they still tend to treat women contemptuously and that is the reason of custodial rape by policemen themselves which happen ever so frequently. In a recent rape case' even the judgement used the words "Women of easy virtue" and the judgement for the rape was biased.

If the police are to act as protectors, there should be better training, better education, right attitude and motivation. The over burdened judicial machinery, complicated enforcement procedures, etc. delay processing of cases.

The evil of dowry continues. In fact it has spread into communities which did not practice before, in spite of the dowry prohibition Act of 1961.

There is some confusion in the interpretation of the word "dowry". Is it the consideration given at the time of marriage or does it also include the gifts given at festival time, child birth etc?

The Sati Prevention Act was passed in 1987 but glorification of Sati continues in States like Rajasthan. The Roop Kanvar case in Deorale is a particular example.

Immoral Traffic Prevention Act of 1956 does not prohibit prostitution altogether. Nor does it give legitimacy to promiscuous sexual activity.

Medical Termination of Pregnancy Act of 1971 has led to amniocentesis and female foeticide. It is believed that 78000 female foeticides are done every year. The State of Maharashtra has passed an act against this.

Indecent Representation of Women's Protection Act was passed in 1986 but the media continues to project women as sex objects. Once the censor board has permitted, the Supreme Court cannot intervene.

Suitable changes in the Indian Penal Code, the Code of Criminal Procedure and the Indian Evidence Act have been made especially for the offence of rape. But judicial process and perceptions continue to be heavily weighed against the victim of rape. The victim has to prove non consent. We find very few rapists get convicted.

Some of the labour laws are never enforced and some are enforced in a mutilated form. In spite of the equal remuneration act of 1976, there is discrimination in promotion, training and transfer on the basis of sex.

Bigamy continues; crimes against women are on the increase With exclusion of lawyers from the family courts, the existing family courts are found to be inadequate.

Suggestions

(1) Changes in the value system are needed. The masses should be educated to perceive that girls and boys are one and the same. This can happen only if traditional values are replaced by progressive ones.

(2) Women are ignorant of the legislations which have been enacted to provide them specific rights. They should be made aware of these rights. Most of the men in the rural areas also are not aware of the legal rights that have been granted to women. They also seem to have negative attitude towards some of the acts such as dowry prohibition, divorce, child marriage and medical termination of pregnancy. Unless basic attitudes of both men and women are changed through educating them, laws cannot be enforced effectively.

(3) Rural men still consider women subservient to men; they have also disapproved granting of equality to women. Deliberate and planned efforts are necessary to accelerate the process of social change.

WOMEN AND CONSUMER PROTECTION RIGHTS

Through the ages, women have played a very important part from behind the scenes. They have influenced policies and they have given directions.

Our country is passing through considerable economic difficulties; prices are high, there is unemployment and there are shortages of essential commodities. Women bear the burden as they are the ones who run the home and provide proper nourishment to the children. Consumer movement can help in particular situation; they can prevent evils such as hoarding, profitteering and black marketing; they can boycott articles which have been acquired by wrong methods. We can counsel ourselves to restrict our wants and curb our desire to buy more than what we require. All the beautiful catchy advertising slogans entice us to buy more and to use more.

One of the directive principles of State policy is that the State shall direct its policy towards securing that the operation of the economic system does not result in the concentration of wealth and means of production to the common detriment. This means the abolition of those economic conditions which ultimately result in the inequality of economic value between man and man. In the fulfilling of their commitment, the State has been passing a series of Acts what are essentially economic as well as welfare legislations. The Monopolies and Restrictive Trade Practices Act of 1969 and the Consumer Protection Act of 1986, are two such legislations. Other acts which have already been passed are as follows:

Sale of Goods Act	..	1930
Drugs and Cosmetic Act	..	1940
Prevention of Food Adulteration Act	..	1954
The Essential Commodities Act	..	1955
Protection of Civil Rights Act		
Insurance Act	..	1938
Electricity Supply Act	..	1948
The Standards of Weights and Measures Act	..	1976, 1985
Environment Protection Act	..	1986

Definition of Consumer

Broadly defined, a consumer is some one who recevies goods

and services in return for a payment either in the form of taxes or in the form of prices. This includes most of the citizens of any civilized country. Right from the moment of birth each individual is a consumer. All human beings are consumers so long as they live and hence consumer problems are human problems.

Consumer Rights

Every consumer has the right

1. to be protected against the marketing of goods which are hazardous to life and property.
2. to be informed about the quality, quantity, purity, potency, standard and price of goods to protect him against unfair trade practices.
3. to be assured, wherever possible, access to an authority of goods at competitive price.
4. to be heard and to be assured that consumers' interest will receive due consideration at appropriate forums.
5. to seek redressal against unfair trade practices or unscrupulous exploitation.
6. to consumer education.

Consumer Protection Movement in India

Factors responsible for evoking the demand for consumer protection are:

— consumer information gap

— consumer exploitation

— product failures

— complexity of legislative controls and goods

— altered pattern of communication

— need for informed participation in problems of development etc.

There has been so much increase in consumer needs and consumer transactions in quality, quality and complexity, hence there is need for information to enable him to make evaluation and decision.

More than 50% of consumers do not know that most of the advertising to-day tries to deceive people rather than inform them hence it is the duty of the Government to provide information.

Consumer information gap due to the new pattern of communication especially mass media, which is manipulated by marketing experts and business stalwarts leads to consumer exploitation. There is failure in both product and service industry. There is confusion over warranties; problems are manifold and arise daily; it is quite impossible for a common citizen to move the court for redressal. There is dearth of laws to contain the price hike. Barring essential commodities and drugs, there is no law to regulate the fixation of prices of the consumable goods. Consumer movement primarily demands a check on price rise in the present atmosphere.

The people below poverty line - about 40% of the population suffer the most from fraud, excessive prices, exhorbitant credit charges, poor quality of merchandise and services. Sale of goods act of 1970 has not been able to protect the consumer against unscrupulous, greedy and dishonest seller. The standards of weights and measures Act has failed to curb the evil of short weighing.

The Bureau of Indian standards made a feeble attempt in ensuring the quality of some consumer goods.

The scheme of Agmark was introduced by the Ministry of Food and Agriculture to ensure the quality of a few food items. The statute to prevent and control the evil of adulteration of goods remains largely unadministered. The drug laboratories which have the duty of certifying drugs leave much room for improvement.

The law controlling the production, levy and distribution of essential commodities and supply of public utility services has been counter productive and has contributed to deterioration in quality and efficiency of services. Nationalisation of some services has not helped either. To-day the customer is in need of adequate protection against not only a private manufacturer or supply of goods and services but also against undertakings run under the auspices of the State Department or Corporations owned and controlled by the State. The growth of the law on the protection of consumers has been haphazard and piece meal. The provisions scattered over a number of unrelated statutes did not ensure adequate protection of a consumer in a particular situation.

Consumer Groups

During the last two decades, a net work of organisations devoted to protection of consumer interest have been developed in urban areas. Realization on the part of several enlightened citizens that the Government with its limited inspecting staff cannot enforce the laws meant for protecting the consumer and the Government's encouragement to form consumer protection organisation have helped the growth of the consumer groups. There are over 180 consumer protection associations on the list of the Government of India. There are some 45 of them in Gujarat, 26 in Karnataka, 23 in Andhra Pradesh, 19 in Tamil Nadu and 13 in Maharashtra. A good many of them are located in cities. Delhi has the highest in number i.e. 14. Rural India does not have a single consumer protection group.

Every group conducts some educational programmes, other methods of operation are research, advocacy, lobbying, litigation and agitation. The specific educational programmes include organising public meetings, lectures, seminars and conferences; publishing literature, guiding, complaining and writing in news papers are also undertaken. Arranging exhibitions demonstrations and providing public forums for individuals are the other action programmes.

These organisations are non political, non profit oriented secular organisations. All of them strive to create critical awareness among consumers. They educate consumers about their rights and responsibilities, realise ecological responsibility and solidarity among consumers.

Some of the Consumer Protection Associations in India are:

Consumer Guidance Society of India (Bombay)

Akil Bharatiya Grahat Panchayat (Hyderabad)

The Citizen's Forum (Hubli)

Voluntary Organisation in the Interest of Consumer Education (VOICE)

Indian Federation and Consumer Organisation (IFCO)

Consumer Education and Research Centre - CERC (Gujarat)

International Movement

The increase in the volume of international trade and commerce has promoted the inter governmental cooperation. The international consumer protection movement has been growing appreciably. Many developing countries face the problem of well coordinated public distribution system. The majority of the consumers are of low income group and they face non-availability of food products and basic commodities of life of acceptable quality at a reasonable price. The consumer protection in developing countries is more of a necesaity than a matter of academic discussion. The essential commodities must be available to the vast majority of the people at a reasonable price, so that they could improve, to some extent, their quality of life and protect against hazardous or adulterated food stuffs. Many international programmes deal with consumer protection and the emphasis is on providing basic goods and services. The U.N. has also given some guidelines, one important guideline regarding international cooperation is the exchange of information on banned and severely restricted products in order to enable importing countries to protect themselves adequately. In the last two decades, many international organisations like FAO, ILO, UNICEF and IOCU (International Organisations of Consumer Union) have been active in the area of consumer protection. UN general assembly's guidelines include physical safety of consumers, protection of economic interests, access to information needed to make choices, satisfactory standards of production, measures to enable consumers to obtain redress etc.

Women and Children as Consumers

The quality of the life of women and children is inter-linked and is the most sensitive indicator of the progress of a given society.

The UN convention on the rights of the child says that the children should have all facilities and opportunities that are necessary for improving the quality of life.

Tamilnadu Profile

Per capita income	..	Rs. 1653 per annum
Per capita monthly expenditure	..	Rs. 103 in rural areas Rs. 176 in urban areas
Infant death	..	18.3%
Infant mortality	..	68 to 1000
Total no. of child working	..	871313

Retention of children in school: By middle school, only 52% are retained, High school, only 27% are retained, Higher Secondary School only 12% are retained.

Destitute children - 27000 street children in Madras alone about 1.5 million chidren are orphans. Mentally retarded = 1 in 800, Physically handicapped 2% (national average 1.8%).

Tamilnadu is the second largest urbanised State.

40% of the population live in urban area countries. 17% of the urban population live in slums.

Sex ratio - 977:1000

Pollution: - Industrial, from tanneries, air pollution due to thermal power stations and automobiles

Adulteration - Hotels run in unhygienic condition - use of toxic colours.

Deforestation - Use of firewood for cooking.

Important issues: Providing potable water, Sewage disposal and Sanitation, Child labour, Female infanticide, Disabled and destitute children.

The recent debut of mass media in the field of advertising consumer goods pose new dangers to the consumer. Gullible consumers are duped into accepting foods of dubious quality; the cut throat competition in prices, reduction sales, free gifts accompanying certain items and other inducements of selling goods of second rate quality - all these have managed to escape MRTP.

The Advertising Standards Council of India has drawn up a code not to use children's pictures for dangerous activities, violent activities, tobacco, paan masala etc.

The wrappers do not contain the information about the product and sometimes they are put in small print which no one notices for e.g.

Nycil - "not suitable for infants is put in very small print.

Tooth paste with flouride - not suitable for children.

Johnson's cotton buds	-	should not be used by children.
Baby soap	-	should not have resin.
Detergents with phosphates	-	banned in other countries but not in India.
Naphthelene balls	-	the vapour can induce nausia and diarrhoea and if swallowed, can cause concussion.
Extra soft pillow	-	can smother a child.
Chemical fumes of paints and synthetics	-	affects children.
Noise pollution	-	above 87 decibels can cause deafness.
Vicks lozenges	-	harmful for children.
Cola, Thums up, Rasna,	-	No nutritional value, contain cafein.
Gripe Water	-	only aniseed water.
Candy with menthol	-	prohibited in other countries for children. Complan,
Boost, Cerelac etc.	-	make tall claims.

food product containing more sodium gluconate, for example 'Maggie noodles' is prohibited in other countries but aggressively advertised in India. Unscrupulous advertisers use contests in T.V. programmes and newspapers. Some advertisements are deceptive and misleading.

Processed food with synthetic preservatives induce behavioural aberrations.

Exaggerated claims are made about glucose powder and protein powders.

Potato wafers are high in sodium and can induce blood pressure. Subtle and covert pressure is put on gullible children - superman toys, G.I. Joes, Barbie dolls etc are example of this pressurisation.

Conclusion

In India, explotation of the people by the people or even by the Government is not a new problem. The politician in the name of serving the country is seen exploiting the society; the administrator in the name of advancing the economic well being, is seen ruthlessly exploiting its precious resources; the seller of goods and services is seen exploiting the customers and so on. All this goes on in the face of constitutional and other laws which aim at curbing and controlling such nefarious tendencies. The desire for rapid material advancement and economic prosperity has commercialised our life on a gigantic scale during the past 40 years. The most painful casualty of this development is the near total collapse of the nation's character and moral fabric. For making huge profits, or becoming rich overnight, all sorts of mal-practices are adopted by traders, businessmen, employers, producers and sellers at the cost of consumers' interest. The plight of the consumer is worst confounded because of her ignorance, illiteracy and weak economic position. A vast majority of consumers in our country are helplessly at the mercy of ruthless exploiters, hoarders, black marketeers and profiteers . To tolerate evil is to spoil the good. To nip the evil in the bud, Consumer Protection, Act of 1986 introduced a new dimension to the concept of law as a tool of social engineering.

The consumers should come together to act against mal-practices of business community. This should become a social movement seeking to augment the rights and powers of buyers in relation to sellers - create the consciousness regarding right to safety, right to be informed, right to choose and right to be heard.

Consumer guidance societies are the need of the hour, they should provide guidance to test the products, consumer resistance is a collective self protection. The method is "refusal to buy"

The Consumer Protection Act of 1986 and its amendments

Its greatest attraction is its convenient channel of justice through District Forum, and its simple, unfettered, non-cumbersome procedure which sets the law in motion with a mere complaint on a plain paper. The act allows only one adjournment so that speedy justice may be possible. Consumer protection courts are set up both at Central and State level. Consumers Disputes Redressal Agencies are the District Forum, state commission and National Commission.

> "There is sufficiency in the World for man's need but not for man's greed". —says *Gandhiji.*

Paper presented by Dr. Mrs. Jaya Kothai Pillai during the Consumer Conference of women at Madurai on 17th Feburary' 94

GANDHI AND NEHRU—ON WOMEN'S RIGHTS

Both Gandhiji and Nehru were against all the social ills of their times with respect to women, namely, child marriage, child widowhood, seclusion of women, enforced widowhood, sati, domestic slavery, polygamy, prostitution, devadasi system and the like. Both of them wanted the Indian women emancipated in the true sense and given opportunities to participate in the nation building activities. We can say that there was some complementarity between the two as the knowledge and experience they gained about women were from the two sections of women, the masses and the classes.

1. The women whom Gandhiji addresses are the ordinary, common, domesticated, uneducated, illiterate, under privileged middle class masses. He knew the real situation of these women, "caged and confined in their home and little courtyards", he says, they had narrow vision and stunted interests, knew nothing beyond the four walls of their homes. The cultural and emotional environment he grew up influenced Gandhiji greatly and he wanted to help create the image of a new woman.

Sita, Damayanthi and Draupadi were the three ideals of Indian womanhood which Gandhiji projected before the women of India. He projected them as symbols of courage, intelligence, perseverance, robust independence and power and not as stereotypes of submission, subserviance, self effacement, helplessness and patience.

He wanted the women to realise that bravery and courage were not the monopoly of men. He wanted the 'abala' or the 'helpless' portrayal of women turned into the 'sabala' or the 'powerful'.

He advised the girls that it is better to remain unmarried rather than being humiliated by marrying men who demanded dowry. According to him, only mutual love and mutual consent should be the necessary conditions for a marriage. He insisted that women must have freedom and dignity in the family and society. He argued that if the husband was not just, the woman had every right to leave him and live separately. His concept of 'chastity' was for both men and women. He said 'pativratha' and 'ekapatnivratha' went together.

Gandhiji believed that women who had been trained in self effacement, self negation and as embodiments of sacrifice were the most suited to take up a non violent struggle and he succeeded in inspiring the traditional house-bound women into entering the satyagraha movement. He admits he learnt the technique of non-violent passive resistance from women, especially, his mother and his wife. He was able to persuade ordinary house wives, like Mira Behn, Gangabehn and Kasturba to rise to the occasion in joining the fight for freedom.

He was keen to get the cultured woman-power involved in the service of the nation. He says "If cultured women of India will make a common cause with the villages, they will produce a silent grand revolution in the village life of India". He pleaded to the Hindu widows that they should come out their shells to serve the poor and the unfortunate and become servants of the nation.

Gandhiji helped to create an atmosphere where celebacy was greatly valued and sexuality controlled. Women were ready to come out of their homes, reside in the ashram and take part in the social and the political struggles without fear of being exploited. This also released women from domestic slavery. According to Gandhiji, "domestic slavery of women is a symbol of our barbarism". He was of the view that domestic work ought not to take the whole of a woman's time and they should be free from this drudgery of cooking. He advocated non-cooked food as a part of the daily diet in the ashram also. so that there would be less cooking.

2. We get some glimpse of Nehru's views on women from his letters to his daughter. His family background, the cultural and social environment in which he grew up and his exposure to western ideas of equality and liberty greatly influenced Nehru's views and the image of women he was familiar with is quite different to that of Gandhiji. In his letters, he says that women should not be educated merely to be an ornament in the drawing room and play the hostess but learn to work outside the home as well. He says,"personally, if I had the chance I would like to have my daughter work in a factory for a year, just as any other worker, as a part of her education".

He felt that Indian women were a matter of pride for the whole country. He says, "I am partial to women of India and the more I have wondered about this great country the more I have felt a ceertain pride in our women folk".

He takes for granted that marriage is a personal affair of two persons. When he addressed the young women graduates ofAllahabad in 1934, he asked the students to fight against the out-of-date customs and laws and bring them in line with modern conditions.

Talking of divorce, he supported the view that mutual consent should be the basis for separation. He did not believe in compelling and forcing people to remain married out of their considerations such as ethics or morals.

In his "Discovery of India" Nehru does talk of the man-made laws and customs and how they have exploited the women and pressurized them to remain dependent and subservient and thus backward. He asks "How can our children grow up into self reliant and efficient citizens of India if their mothers are not themselves self reliant and efficient".

3. Both Gandhiji and Nehru saw education as an essential instrument for enabling women to uphold their natural rights. Gandhiji believed in women's equal legal and political status but he advocates a difference in the curriculum for men and women. He says "True, they are equals in life but their functions differ". He continues "It is woman's right to rule the home. Man is master outside it. Man is the earner, woman saves and spends. Woman looks after the feeding of the child. She shapes its future, she is responsible for building the character. She is her children's educator and hence mother to the nation". Hence he wants the girls to be taught the management of the home, nursing and care of children.

He also says "Unless women cease to be a mere means of pleasure or cooks to us and come to be our life companions, equal partners in the battle of life, share in our joys and sorrows, all our efforts are doomed to failure".

Thus we can see that Gandhiji wants women as equal partners and have a good influence on the children.

There is a little contradiction where he says that no vocation is exclusively reserved for one sex only and challenges the idea of rigid division of labour between the sexes. May be it was too advanced those days to think that men can also share in the caring of children at home.

Gandhiji wants the women to seek justice and not favours. He was not in favour of any reservation for women and he warns them against depending on patronage. He says "our women should become to us what Uma was to Shankar, Sita to Rama and Damayanthi to Nala".

4. Nehru's circle of women were those who had played an important role in the struggle for women. Many of them had stood out by their ability, capacity for organisation and sacrificing for a cause. He was very proud of these women and he says that some of them could be rated high in any assembly of women all over the world.

He says "If you want me to tell you what a nation is like, or what a social organisation is like, tell me the position of women in that country"

Nehru was keen that women should have equal rights as well as duties and they should contribute equal to men in nation building. Nehru agrees with professional thinkers like Bertrand Russell, Carlyle, Ruskin and Shaw in fighting the Victorian ideal of male superiority over women .

5. We are able to get a good, clear picuture of Gandhiji's views on women as he himself has written to women, on women and about women in 'Young India' and 'Harijan'.

We can find Nehru's views on women , only as scattered and casual remarks in his writings. Hence it is difficult, to get a clear, complete piture of his views on various aspects of women. But it can be confidently said that both Gandhiji and Nehru believed in complete equality of men and women in all aspects - economic, social, legal, political and moral.

References

M.K. Gandhi - The Role of Women, ed. Anand Hergorani, Bharatiya Vidya Bhavan, Bombay, 1964.

M.K. Gandhi - An Autobiography—The Navjeevan Trust, 1983.

Geoffrey Ash - Gandhi - A Study in Revolution - Asia Publishing House, 1968.

The Collected Works of Mahatma Gandhi - Navjeevan Trust, 1982.

Eleanor Morton - The Women in Gandhi's life, Dodd, Mead & Co, 1953.

Madhu Kishwar - Gandhi and Women, Manushi Prakashan, 1986.

S.R. Bakshi - Gandhi and Status of Women. Criterion Publications, 1987.

Selected Works of "Jawaharlal Nehru - Orient Longmans.

Paper sent by Dr. Mrs. J.K. Pillai to the National Seminar on "The Complementarity of Gandhi and Nehru - Its relevance, Today and Tomorrow" held at Gandhigram Rural Institure, 27th August, 1989.

SOCIAL AND ECONOMIC DEVELOPMENT OF WOMEN IN THE LAST FOUR DECADES

Background

In the years before Independence, the Indian Economy was characterised by a large undeveloped primitive agriculture interspersed with some segments of a lopsided semideveloped industrial structure which was a direct consequence of the colonial rule. The growth rate of national income between 1901-1946 was only 1.2%, 0.3% for agricultural production and 2.0% for industrial production. According to 1951 figures per capita income in India was fifty times lower than that of USA, 13 times lower than that of U.K. and it was the lowest in comparison to all the 54 under developed countries. A vast majority of Indians lived in appalling poverty. Out of a total labour force of 170 million people, in 1950, about 8 million people were unemployed and 15-20 million under employed. In the educational front, India was behind these countries by about 80-100 years.

"Indian women as a whole, were much worse off than men. The women were less literate, more unemployed, less visible in the authority structure, more prone to diseases and suffered more from barriers of customs and patriarchal norms and values. "According to the Census of 1951, literacy among the females was 7.87 as against 24.88% for males. Expectation of life at birth for females was 31.7 years as against 32.4 years for males. Sex ratio, which was 972 females per 1000 males in 1901 had come down to 946 females per 1000 males. The mean age at marriage for males was 19.8 and females, 15.4 years. In 1951, enrolment of boys in the primary stage was 55% of the population in the corresponding age group and for girls it was only 20.1%. At the middle stage 4.6% girls enrolled as against 20.8% of boys and in the secondary stage, for every 100 boys, only 16 girls enrolled. Enrolment of women in university education was about 11 for every 100 men; of the women workers, 76.8% were in the category of agricultural labourers and cultivators. The sub-committee of the National Planning Committee appointed to deal with the place of women in the planned economy of India in 1947 stated "The picture which we now envisage is that of men and women, comrades of the road, going forward together, the child joyously shared by both. Such a reality we feel cannot but raise the manhood and womanhood of any nation". The importance of the role of women in the planned economy of the country was recognised and given considerable thought by the early planners.

Jawaharlal Nehru in his foreward to Social Welfare in India (1958) states "Women in India have a background of history and tradition behind them which is inspiring. It is true however, that they have suffered much from various kind of suppression and all these have to go so that they can play their full part in the life of the nation".

As soon as India attained Independence, the popular government planned to create a democratic, just and prosperous society through constitutional and legal reforms, planned development based on a mixed economy and state support to welfare activities. All these three steps have had their impact on the economic and social development of women too.

The preamble to the Constitution of India resolved to secure to all its citizens—"Social, economic and political justice, liberty of thought, expression, belief, faith and worship, equality of status and opportunities, dignity of the individual and the unity of the nation". Indian women are entitled to these rights just as men are. Some of the women specific directive principles are— free and compulsory education for all children up to the age of fourteen, right to an adequate means of livelihood, equal pay for equal work, maternity relief etc.

The process of planned economic development in India began with the launching of the first five year plan in April 1951. The central purpose of planning has been to achieve a rapid rate of economic development with a view to raise the levels of living of the Indian people. The major objectives of the plans have been: stepping up the rate of economic growth, modernization of economy, achieving self reliance and promoting social justice.

Women in the Five Year Plans

The First Five Year Plan (1951-56) stated that the Central objectives of the plan was to initiate a process of development which would raise the living standards and open out to people new opportunities for a richer and more varied life. With very meagre resources at its command, the first plan was largely confined to agriculture, irrigation and power. It had to confront low rate of economic growth, mounting population pressure, backward agriculture and an insignificant industrial development of over half a century besides the imbalances created by the world war and partition of the country.

This plan gave due attention to social services like health, education, sanitation, housing and rehabilitation to build up human capital. The plan recognised the problems of high infant and maternal mortality and undertook to develop school feeding schemes, maternity centres and child health centres. The Central Social Welfare Board was established by the Government in 1953 with a nationwide programme of grants in aid for promoting development of women and children. The Board had its counterparts in the states and they provided assistance to voluntary agencies for improving and developing welfare programmes. This led to the growth of a number of women's organisations and provided status and activity to many of the erstwhile active women social workers. Proliferation of mahilamandals is a striking phenomenon of this period. This plan was able to achieve the targets, both in agricultural production and industrial production; per capita income recorded an increase of 11% and per capita consumption showed an improvement of about 8%. The price level came down by 13%. This plan was able to bring about a marked improvement in economic development as well as welfare services.

The Second Plan (1955-61) aimed to achieve rapid industrialisation. It emphasised maximum production, full employment, attainment of economic equality and social justice. Since agriculture was given low priority, its slow growth acted as a limiting factor in the industrial development as well. This plan performance fell short of the targets. There was an increase in price level, the performance in employment generation was not satisfactory. The failure of monsoon, costlier inputs, unrealistic planning etc. were the reasons for the poor performance of the plan.

But as far as women's issues are concerned this plan persisted in welfare approach. It recognised the need for organisation of women as workers, that women should be protected against injurious work, should receive maternity benefits and creches should be established for children in work places. It also recommended speedy implementation of the principle equal pay for equal work and provision of training to enable women compete for higher jobs.

In 1961, at the end of this plan period, it was reported that in the organised sector, due to the necessity of providing welfare measures, many of the employees were reluctant to employ women and the participation rate of the female working force in comparison with the males declined. The participation rate of the female working force stood at 27.96 as against 57.12 for males. Further, as women were not encouraged to take technical training or on-the-job training, modernization of some industries like textiles, led to the displacement of women.

In the areas of health and education there was some progress. The literate percentage of females increased to 12.95 but still low, as compared to males, which was 34.44%. Expectation of life at birth in 1961 was 40.6 for females as against 41.9 for males. The decline in the sex ratio continued and in 1961 it stood at 941 females per 1000 males. There was a spurt in the enrolment of girls in the educational system, the number of girls in school system being 42 per 100 boys and 16.2 girls per 100 men at the University stage.

The Third Plan (1961-66) : This plan incorporated the objectives of the prèvious plans and added self sufficiency in foodgrains as one more objective. It sought to achieve self reliance by reducing dependence on external assistance. It focussed on expansion of girls' education as a strategy for women's development. Efforts on providing condensed course for adult women in health, nutrition and family planning were continued.

This plan also fell short of the targets in economic development. Higher rate of growth of population prevented any rise in the level of per capita income. Widespread drought conditions led to fall in agricultural outputs. Sino Indian conflict, Indo-Pak war and the consequent disruptions in foreign aid slowed down industrial production and all this led to inflation and rise in prices. The backlog of unemployment could not be cleared. However, the spread of education and training facilities were substantial during this plan period and a number of benefits were provided to the poorer sections of the society. But these efforts could not mitigate the widespread poverty.

The shape of economy at the end of the Third Plan was so bad that the fourth five year plan could not be launched in 1966 and annual plans repalced this five year plan in the next three-year period. During these three years (1966-69) the unfinished task of the third plan was continued and though there was some recovery in production levels, inflation could not be controlled. However, with the introduction of green revolution, the confidence of the people in planning was restored.

The Fourth Plan (1969-1974) recognised the importance of agriculture as a key factor in economic development and schemes of irrigation were assigned an importance place. The plan continued the emphasis on women's education. The outlay on family planning was stepped up, high priority was given to immunisation of pre-school children, supplementory diet for children, expectant and nursing mothers. Otherwise in general, this plan also did not achieve the major growth targets. Attaining self sufficiency in foodgrains did not materialise. Indo-Pak War of 1971 caused a sharp dislocation of economic activity and severe drought conditions led to increase in food prices.

According to the census of 1971, the literacy percentage increased from 12.95 (1961) to 18.69%. The literacy percentage of males increased to 39.56. Expectation of life at birth for females was 44.7 as compared to 46.4 for males. Sex ratio continued to decline, the figure for 1971 being 930 per 1000 males, Enrolment of girls in the education system continued to rise in the school system there were 54 girls for every 100 boys and in the university system, 21.9 girls per 100 boys enrolled. Thus the rate of progress of education of girls was very slow and there was wide gap between the education of boys and girls at all stages. Participation rate of female working force declined for 27.96 to 11.87 as against 52.51 for males, displacement of women continuing. The middle class educated women fared better, they assumed a new role as earning partners and they developed career interests. But as the several division of labour between men and women in the family was very pronounced, these women had to carry on the burden of two full time jobs.

The Fifth Plan (1974-79): The Fifth Plan's major objective was removal of poverty and attainment of self reliance. The declaration of emergency, and then change in the government in the centre upset the plan programmes and this plan was operated as annual plans. The Janata Government modified some of the priorities and adult education and functional literacy received more emphasis. Functional literacy programmes to train women in the age group 15-45 in the functions of a house-wife, including child care, nutrition, health care and home economy were stressed.

Thus in all the five plans, the priorities assigned to women's development programmes were mainly education, health and some aspects of welfare. The committee constituted to examine the social status of women by the Government of India in 1971 reported in December 1974. This report highlighted the following:

1. The majority of women were still not enjoying the rights and opportunities gvaranteed to them by the Constitution.
2. Increase in the incidence of dowry was lowering the status of women.
3. Women were still ignorant of their legal rights regarding marriage, divorce, adoption, inheritance and maternity benefits.
4. Child marriage was still continuing and there was high incidence of suicide among young married women.
5. Though there has been tremendous increase in the enrolment of girls in formal education since independence, there was still a wide gap between enrolment of boys and girls and the proportion of girls in the relevant age groups in the school system was far below the constitution's target of universal education up to the age of 14.
6. There was great disparity of educational progress of girls between urban and rural areas, region to region, among communities, religions etc. The drop out ratio was very high among girls.
7. The declining sex ratio over several decades, high female maternal and infant mortality rates revealed the neglect of general public health services, maternity and child health services.
8. The impact of transition to modern economy has excluded a large number and proportion of women from active participation in the productive processes. The majority of those who participate have no equal treatment, security of employment and humane conditions of work.

This report recommended suitable measures for improving the status of women.

A major outcome of the report was the National Plan of Action in 1976 which identified areas of health, family planning, nutrition, education, employment, legislation and social welfare for formulating and implementing action programmes for women and called for planned intervention to improve the condition of women in India.

Women's Welfare and Development Bureau was set up under the Ministry of Social Welfare in 1976 to act as a nodal point to initiate measures for women's development.

The CSWI report of 1975 greatly influenced the Sixth Plan. For the first time there was a shift from welfare to development approaches for women. This plan recognised women's lack of access to resources as an important factor impeding their development. As the basic unit of development programming was still the 'family' and not the 'woman' women benefitted very little.

During the Sixth Plan period (1980-85): A variety of programmes, were taken up under different sectors of development to ameliorate the working conditions of women and to raise their economic and social status. Vocational Training Centres and Industrial Training Institutes exclusively meant for women were set up. The Integrated Rural Development Programme accorded priority to women heads of households, one-third of the beneficiaries under TRYCEM were women, and a new scheme called 'Development of women and Children in Rural Areas' (DWACRA) was started in 1982-83. Training in a chosen economic activity such as weaving, fish vending, rope making, brick making-candle making, baking etc along with the necessary infrastructure was provided.

Non formal education centres were set up exclusively for girls. To boost enrolment in primary classes, early childhood education centres were set up as adjuncts to primary schools. Higher rates of scholarship were given to girls, belonging to scheduled tribes and scheduled classes. Separate Universities for women were established in Tamilnadu and AndhraPradesh. The Ministry of Social Welfare implemented a programme called "Functional Literacy for Adult Women". Under the scheme "Science and Technology for Women" a wide spectrun of activities such as smokeless chullahs, solar cookers, bio-gas plants, water purificater system etc. were taken up. To reduce drudgery of women's day to day activities, improved agricultural implements, better methods of sheep rearing, wool spinning, post harvest activities, food processing, fish processing, pearl culture etc. were taken up.

Nutritional intervention to pregnant and nursing mothers belonging to weaker sections was given high priority under the ICDS programme. Hostels for working women, training cum production centres for women, assistance to women in distress etc. were some of the schemes for which financial assistance was given to voluntary organisations.

In the Seventh Plan (1985-90): The basic approach was to inculcate confidence among women to bring about an awareness of their own potential for development as also of their rights and privileges. The plan emphasised the need to open new avenues of work for women and proclaim them as a crucial resource for the development of the country. Besides access of women to land, support through credit marketing, training in skills and management were included.The plan saw the need to organise women workers so that they could demand their rights for services. The plan also acknowledged the long hours spent by women within the household as well as their labour in farms or family business.

The Government of India constituted a separate department in the Ministry of Human Resource Development, for the development of women and children. This department plans and executes programmes for women besides monitoring the programmes meant for women in other ministries and departments.

The thrust of the various programmes are on providing employment and income generation services, education and training services, support services, general awareness services and legal support services. Women's development corporations have been set up by a few State Governments for training and employment of women from weaker sections of society. The Department of Women and Child Development has floated many programmes like providing short-stay homes for women and girls in moral danger, counselling, medical care, psychiatric guidance, preventive rehabilitative services to women and children who are victims of atrocities and exploitations. The total outlay on the women specific schemes in the VIIth Plan is 2.4%.

The Department of Women and Child Development set up a core group to evaluate the impact of developmental plans and programme on Indian women and review the policies and programme and draft perspective plans for 1988-2000 A.D. This document was released in October 1988.

The overall approach of this National Perspective Plan is to perceive women in a holistic manner. This plan has made sectoral reviews of the situation of women in Rural Development, Employment, Supportive Services, Education, Health, Legislature, Political participation and Media and Communication and suggested inter linkages and converging strategies. The specific recommendation of this plan is that well articulated national policies with specific objectives should be formulated for increasing the participation of women in developmental plans. These should aim at the creation of productive employment for women as well as provision of services to women so as to enable them to participate more fully in economic growth and social progress.

This plan, recognises the importance of women's potential as a human resource, and the most critical imput for development as training. The establishment of an apex body for women's training in the country is urged and this body would be responsible for reorientation and sensitization of the administrative machinery at all levels to the issues of women in development. This apex body would be responsible for revamping the existing content/methodology and monitoring the training of catalyst functionaries.

The plan also recommends that a commissioner for women's rights should be appointed for the enforcement of law to ensure women's rights. The unpaid work of women in the household and outside and its value was to be taken into account and a conceptual clarity on 'work' and 'non work' and their economic value should be examined.

A reservation of 30% seats in all elected bodies, as a transitionary measure is necessary to ensure that women have the opportunity to enjoy equal political status with men.

The plan reiterates strengthening of minimum needs programme, women's access to productive resources such as land and credit inputs, review of property laws to ensure women's access to property rights, women oriented wasteland development programmes of social forestry, skill training for women in agriculture, animal husbandry and other related employment, unionising of women, expansion of insurance cover, maternity and other benefits, special training programme for rural women entrepreneurship, appropriate techno logy for drudgery reduction and enhancing productivity, supportive services for women in distress, legal aid centres, counselling centres, creche/day care facilities, special cells to enforce legislation on job security, working condition, minimum wages, equal pay for equal work etc which should be extended to unorganised sectors, use of media to create awareness for women's education and their active role in economic, political development of the nation, adult education programmes, banning amniocentesis for sex determination, strengthening ICDS programmes to ensure girl child's equal access to health care, sex and family planning education in schools, colleges and universities encouraging folk media for reaching women in rural areas, uniform civil code for all citizens etc.

To sum up, the government articulated the norm of equality through the Constitution and tried to achieve the goal by enacting laws for ushering social change, planned economic development and strengthening voluntary agencies for welfare activities. In effect free India provided a basic framework for possible improvement of women's status. There have been conscious efforts to change the position of women form inequality to equality.

Some of the achievements in improving the status of women are, the expectation of life at birth has improved from 44.7 in 1971 to 52.9 years in 1981 and 55.9 years in 1981. The sex ratio has registered a slight rise from 930 to 933 per thousand males in 1981 but has come down to 927 female for every 1000 males in 1991. The average age at marriage for girls has gone up to 18.3 years as against 17.2 years in 1971, the focus in the programmes for women has shifted from welfare to development, there is more involvement of women in the planning and implementation processes at all levels, efforts for removing sexist bias and promotion of the value of equality through school curricula, beneficiary oriented schemes specially for women, several legislative enactments and amendments to protect the interest of women etc.

As against this rosy picture, there are several dismal factors too.

Hardly 25% of our women are literate; among the rural women, 83% are illiterate; over 90% of the women work in unorganised sectors, where no child care or maternity benefits are available; number of unemployed girls who have completed school has risen to 51 lakhs; 65% of the pregnant women are found to be anaemic; infant mortality rate in the first year of birth is about 10%, children dying of malnutrition before the age of 5 is about 40%.

The menace of dowry, violence against women, sexual harassment, damaging portrayal of women in the media, infanticide, foeticide etc are growing.

In many cases, employment per se has not improved women's status as women do not have control over the productivity of labour. Less than 1% of the property is owned by women.

"There is continued inequality and vulnerability of women in all sectors—economic, social, political, education and health care, nutrition and legal" states the perspective plan.

The Government have offered welfare schemes for women; they have floated anti poverty programmes. They have enacted legislation to safeguard women's rights. The Government policies can only facilitate the process. It is the women themselves, who should become conscious of their inequality and oppression and seize all available opportunies to improve their status. It is heartening to note that during the last two decades, women's Voluntary Organisations have been quite active taking up issues like violence against women, rape, dowry death, sati glorification, media distortion of women's image, problem of working women, dual burden of women, gender discrimination etc and in general a widespread awareness is being created among men and women at all levels and it is hoped that during the 21st century, women would march towards equality in the real sense.

References

Bhargava B.K. - Planning and Economic Policy, 1984.

Gupta A.K. - (Ed.) Women and Society.

Sharma K. Hussain S. and Saharya A. - Women in Focus (1984) 1986.

Status of Women in India - Report of the National Committee on the Status of Women, ICSSR, 1974.

National Perspective Plan for Women 1988-2000 A.D - Department of Women and Child Development, Ministry of Human Resource Development, Government of India, 1988.

Paper sent by Dr. Mrs. J.K. Pillai, Vice-Chancellor of Mother Teresa Women's University, Kodaikanal.

LIBERATION OF WOMEN IN THE INDIAN CONTEXT EDUCATIONAL IMPLICATIONS AT THE COLLEGE STAGE

As a majority of human kind, women clearly comprise the largest group in the world. Women constitute the only group which is treated unequally as a whole but whose members live in greater intimacy with their oppressors than with each other". (Chage, 1977).

Women's social, economic and political status is lower than that of men in all countries be it USA, USSR, UK, India or China. Their social status in a given society depends upon the particular role assigned to women and the social attitudes towards that role. It is true that women do enjoy better position in some societies than in some others.

Why have women occupied a subordinate position in society? How can the variations of this subordination be explained?

The origin of female subordination and how women were neglected to a lower status have been analysed by various approaches and various theories have been formulated. The three major approaches are radical feminism, socialist feminism and moderate feminism. The radical feminists believe that society is primarily divided on the basis of sex and women's subjugation is due to sexual oppression by men. According to them male supremacy is the oldest, most basic form of domination. Women should be freed from biological limitations by technological developments such as reliable birth control measures, artificial reproduction etc. The end goal, according to this school is not just the elimination of male privilege but of sex distinction itself.

The socialist feminism or Marxist analysis has located the origin of female subordination in the family i.e., in the development of surplus wealth due to the phenomenon of private property. The family is the result of private property in the means of production and complete equality of women is possible only when private property is abolished. So they advocate class struggle which will lead to the abolition of private property. Though the status of women in socialist countries is better than their counterparts in the capitalist countries, even in the socialist societies, women do not enjoy equal status with men. Soviet women are still responsible for the full burden of house work and child rearing. The family system continues to be strong in these countries also.

Both, radical feminism and socialist feminism believe that revolution is necessary to liberate women and help her to attain equality with men. Radical feminists plead for sexual revolution and social feminists work for economic and political revolution.

The moderate feminists do not find it necessary to resort to revolution but they believe in social reform and a change of social values and attitudes. According to this school, the inferior position of women is due to cultural and psychological factors. J.S. Mill, one of the earliest thinkers of this approach says that the subjugation of women was the product of age long custom and was not the proof of any inherent inferiority in them. Bertrand Russel and Mahatma Gandhi belonged to this school and they wanted women to be educated, brought out of the four walls of the home and enjoy equal status with men. This school advocates that women should demand legal protection against sex discrimination; they should fight unjust social customs against women and change the prevalent attitudes and values. All social scientists accept the main postulate that woman is not biologically inferior and her lower social status to that of man is man made.

In India, radical and socialist feminist groups are of recent origin and they are few and scattered whereas, moderate feminism has a fairly long history in India.

Historical Setting: In India in the Pre Aryan Society, property was communal, there was no caste or class distinction within the tribe. According to Kosambi (1965) "agriculture was the monopoly of women. She was the first potter and weaver" Patil (1982) says that the system of matriarchy prevailed in different parts of the continent before 400 B.C. and that in some parts, women were the rulers.

The rulership of 'Alli' in the coastal islands is well known to the Tamils. Historians have established that women in early vedic days in India enjoyed an equal status with men in the different spheres of life. There were as many as twenty women who composed the hymns of the Rigveda. Women philosophers were called Brahma Vadinis and we come across a galaxy of learned women such as Ghosha, Romasa, Lopamudra, Gargi, Vachaknavi, Aitreyi and Maitreyi, Kautilya's Arthasastra talks of women soldiers armed with bows and arrows.

Individuals bore names derived from their mothers; says Gargi. There is no mention of burning or burial of widows; on the other hand we come across many names such as Sita Draupadi, Savitri and Rukmini who chose their life partners by Swayamvara. In the Tamil country also, we see a similar picture during the early Christian era, i.e., the Sangam age. There was no early marriage of girls and they were given certain independence in their choice of their mates.

Many Sangam poems are attributed to women scholars and we hear of as many as 37 lady poets.

In course of time, for a vriety of reasons, matriarchal system slowly disappeared. As Aryans moved towards the east and south, they married non-Aryan women to establish their victory and thus women was slowly becoming more of a possession. Non-Aryan women, not familiar with Sanskrit, became ineligible to participate in religious sacrifices and in course of time all women lost the privilege to Vedic studies. Upanayanam for girls became a mere formality and then slowly disappeared. Women came to be equated with the sudras who were also ineligible for Vedic studies. Not having the privilege of education, early marriage for girls became an established practice by 100 A.D. Marriage by choice became non existent; women's status was lowered and she became subordinate to man—father, husband or son.

Evidence of dowry system is found after 200 A.D. In Brahma Purana we come across Sursena presenting his daughter with gold, Cows, horses and ornaments. We also come across the system of seclusion of women in Brahma Purana. Women were advised not to see the face of a man other than her husband. We see the influence of the Dharma Sastras of the north in Tamil Nadu also in the deterioration of the position of women.

The influence of Jainism and Budhism which believed that women was a source of distraction from piety was also another reason for despising the women and women being looked down upon.

During the Moghul period, purdah system became well established; emphasis on women's chastity increased; strict restrictions were imposed on widows. Thus by medieval period upper caste and appereless Hindu women became completely subordinated to her husband. The middle classes emulated the upper classes and women came to be considered as inferior, men's possession, secluded in inner quarters, losing their equality, freedom and privilege of education.

During the 19th century, as western education and western thoughts influenced, more and more educated Indians made several efforts to improve the conditions of women in all parts of the country. During the early part of the 19th century attempts were made by social reformers like Ram Mohan Roy to, abolish sati, abolish child marriage and allow widow remarriage. During the mid 19th century, education of women received greater attention and this led to the struggle for political rights and adult suffrage to women. Women leaders started a campaign for the removal of ban on entering legislatures and won it. The Congress under Gandhiji's leadership demanded unconditional women's suffrage and independent India granted legal equality to women and guaranteed political equality. The constitution of India has incorporated complete equality of men and women, no discrimination on grounds of sex; equality of opportunity in employment, equal pay for equal work, humane conditions of work, maternity relief, eligibility to electoral rolls, right to vote and hold public life (articles 14, 15, 16, 39, 325 and 326). Since independence, our laws have changed and changed with tremendous speed. The Hindu code bill is a real charter for emancipation of women. The Education Commission (1964-66) has rightly observed "In the modern world; the role of women goes beyond the home and bringing up of children. In the struggle for freedom, women fought side by side with men. This equal partnership will have to continue in the fight against hunger, poverty, ignorance and ill health". What are the implications of this struggle for liberation on higher education?

Due to the efforts of social reformers and missionaries, women's education slowly gained ground and schools all over the country were started. Training colleges for women were established and women were trained to become teachers in girls schools. In 1883, for the first time, two women graduated from Calcutta University. By 1902, as many as 177 girls enrolled in liberal arts colleges and 87 in professional colleges. Women took to nursing and medicine. During the first half of the 20th century girls enrolment in higher education increased enormously.

By 1950-57, there were 40,000 girls at the college level and by 1965-66 2,70,000. Though this looks spectacular, as compared to boys, there were only 14 girls in colleges for every 100 boys in 1950-51 and 25 girls per 100 in 1965-66. In the field of professional education, as against 87 girls in 1901, there were 5,000 girls in 1950-51 and around 50,000 in 1965-66.

Though there was phenomenal expansion in women's education, in the first half of the 20th century, the purpose of education was still to produce "good mothers and wives".

Karve, the outstanding educationist who was responsible for establishing the exclusive SNDT Women's University in Maharashtra believed that the place of women was distinct from that of men and that education should equip women for this place. Gandhiji also was of similar views. He wanted women to be educated in domestic affairs and child rearing. These views influenced the policy makers of post-independent India and the National Committee on Women's Education also confirmed that the main purpose of women's education is to train them to be modern, educated, conscious and skilled housewives and mothers.

Women's associations also stressed the role of the mother and housewife. That there should be no barrier in the way of women who wished to embark on professional or public causes following the ordinary course of study in colleges and universities was raised by more and more professional women leaders. More women wanted to opt for courses in Law, Medicine, Engineering, Fine Arts and Social Sciences. With spread of higher education among women, the interests of women have been widening and their activities have been expanding.

But even today, the concept of equality is being defined within the framework of 'Indianness'. Educated women and men still beieve that women may take gainful occupations outside the home but independent careers should not disturb family life. "Fatihful and uncomplaining wives' is the Indian demand.

In spite of more women taking advantages of higher education, there is discrimination in social, economic and political spheres. The number of women in decision making bodies such as Parliament and State assemblies is negligible. The participation of women in labour force has been declining through the years. The rate of suicide among female is more than among the males. Instances of rape and bride burning have increased. Single women are not safe in Indian society. Women's inferior status is legitimized by the state in school text-books and media. Her sufferings are glorified under the pretext of strengthening traditional values.

Suggestions : Education should develop consciousness among women for their rights and the necessity to raise their status. More and more women should be trained in media management, as editors, columnists, reporters, producers etc.

Courses for the both sexes should include employment oriented subjects as well as family life, nutrition and responsible parenthood. Diversified vocational programmes of all types should be offered at the collegiate stage. There should be no age restriction for women either for continuing studies or coming back to work. Co-education and mixed training groups should be actively encouraged. Popularization of family planning courses, organization of child welfare and day care centres, working women's hostels, inexpensive labour saving devices, central food facilities etc., would enhance women's participation in social processes.

Above all, a psychic revolution in the minds of both men and women is needed. Education must make a deliberate, planned and sustained effort to inculcate equality of sexes as a major value and instil mutual understanding and respect for each other.

References

Agnew Vijay — Elite Women in Indian Politics New Delhi: Vikas Publishing House, 1979.

Beg Tara Ali (Ed.) — Women in Ancient India, Delhi: The Publication Division, 1958.

Chofe William — Women and Equality, Oxford University Papers, 1977.

Desouza Alfred (Ed.) — Women in Contemporary India, New Delhi: Manohar Publications, 1975.

Ghurye, I — Vedic India, Bombay: Popular Prakasam, 1979.

Hamilton Roberta — The Liberation of Women, London, George Allen and Unwin, 1978.

Kosambi, D.D. The Culture and Civilization of Ancient Indian Historical Outlines, London: Routledge and Kegan Paul, 1965.

Patil, Sharad Dasa-Sudia Slavery, New Delhi: Allied Publishers, 1982.

Pillai, J.K. Educational System of the Ancient Tamils, Madras: Tirunelveli Saiva Siddhantha Works Publishing Society, 1972.

Pillai, J.K. "Dual Role of Women" in New Frontiers of Education.

Shah Kalpana Women's Liberation and Voluntary Action, Delhi: Ajantha Publications, 1984.

2

RURAL WOMEN

Women and Rural Development

A Profile of Female Agricultural Labourers in Tamil Nadu

Problems of Women Head-loaders in Kodaikanal

Entrepreneurial Development of Rural Women

The New Economic Policy and Women's Development

WOMEN AND RURAL DEVELOPMENT

In the newsletter of Summer/Spring 1987 of INSTRAW, the United Nation's International Research and Training Institute for the Advancement of Women, there was a poster with the following words:

"We are more than half the numbers

We do more than half the work

We are more than half the poor

We have more than half the love

We have more than half the dreams"

This is the cry of the rural women of the third world countries.

In India, percentage of rural women to the total female population is 80.5. A time disposition study on 'Work participation by the landless poor' by Indira Devi (1983) reveals that the average number of working hours per day for a rural woman is 15 to 18 and of this, 8 hours is used for domestic work alone. Almost all the rural women fall below the poverty line. Women not only work in the farm- Sowing, weeding, transplanting, harvesting, threshing, winnowing, grass cutting, feeding and milking animals, poultry activities, fetching water, collecting fuel and fodder, they also have to cook, wash, feed, nurse and look after the family. Unfortunately, all this work has remained largely invisible to the planners.

The conference report of UN Decade for Women, Copenhagan (1980) says that "Total development includes development in political, economic, social, cultural and other dimensions of human life as also the physical, moral, intellectual and cultural growth of the human person". Women's development should be seen as an essential component in every dimension of development.

Rural development should lead to improvement of all aspects of rural life—healthy individual, clean environment, provision of minimum essentials, such as clean drinking water, nutritious food, roof over the head, less drudgery of work, adequate income, etc.

What is the profile of rural women in India?

Profile

She is poor, ignorant, illiterate, superstitious and suppressed.

She has low access to information and knowledge.

Her skill level is low.

She has low access to income generating assets.

She has low accesss to new employment opportunities.

She is unorganized, unrepresented and politically powerless.

She has low access to leadership position.

She has multiple burdens.

She is over worked but gets low returns for her work.

Most of her work is invisible.

She has no information of her rights.

But she is a producer, a farmer a worker in the household.

She is an active participant in development.

We need to help her to improve her skills, her earning power and educational level.

She needs access to science and technology to reduce the drudgery of labour in her day-to- day household work.

She needs better wages and better price for her produce.

She needs land ownership rights and credit facilities.

She needs to be trained in organizing production, marketing and management.

She needs to be organised for collective actions and to strengthen her bargaining power.

The strategies that have been used in rural development in education, extension and technology.

Though the enrolment of girls in primary schools has increased from 25% (1951) to 60% in 1981, the dropout rate among rural girls is high—70% of the dropouts are girls. Extension activities have so far catered more to males. Women have been ignored as they have not been able to comprehend innovations. Extension activities of the gram-sevikas have been more oriented towards welfare tasks, health, nutrition and child care.

It is also found that technology has affected rural women's

employment. According to a report of S. Acharya (1984), a typical rice mill displaces 1500 women's jobs and creates 45 jobs for men.

Mechanization has hit women's employment in post-harvest operations in rice areas.

Cold storage plants have displaced thousands of fisherwomen from their jobs of fish processing and selling.

Using of biogas for rural industry has adversely affected women's cooking energy needs.

Seriousness about integration of women in the developmental programmes started in 1980, with the Sixth Five Year Plan, after the report on the status of women was published and a lot of information was made available on the multiple roles of women, their development and training needs. Inadequate focus on women by the earlier plans can be attributed to the lack of appreciation of the role of women and lack of a proper perspective.

The major thrust of the Sixth Five Year Plan was economic uplift of women through greater opportunities for employment, imparting of new skills and upgrading existing skills.

Today, 17 departments of 8 ministries have 45 training schemes for the benefits of women. 31 training programmes provide training in skills for employment in all sectors.

The Integrated Rural Development Plan (IRDP) focus on the eradication of rural poverty. 30% of the beneficiaries are women.

The scheme of Development of Women and Children in Rural Areas (DWCRA) enables women to undertake schemes of self employment for incremental income.

One third of the beneficiaries of the programme of Training Rural Youth for Self Employment (TRYCEM) are women and about 47 lakhs of women have been trained so far.

National Rural Employment Programme (NREP), Rural Landless Employment Guarantee Programme (RLEGP), Self Employment Porgramme for Women, etc. provide new job opportunities in the area of agriculture, social forestry, fisheries, minor irrigation works, handloom, khadi and village industries.

Non governmental agencies such as Self Employed Women's Association (SEWA) of Ahmedabad, Community Health and Development Programme (CHAD) of CMC, Vellore, All India Women's Conference, Working Women's Forum, Young Women's Christian Assoication, etc. are also successfully operating developmental programmes for women.

The talent and potential of all—both men and women— are necessary for the total development of a country. Involvement and integration of women in development is vital for economic and social success.

A PROFILE OF FEMALE AGRICULTURAL LABOURERS IN TAMIL NADU

Agriculture is the major economic activity for women. According to the census of 1971, 80% of women workers were found in agriculture and they constituted 87% of the female work force in rural areas. Agricultural workers are classified into two categories, viz. cultivators and labourers. Labourers include casual daily wage labourers, seasonal migrant labourers, contract workers and bonded labourers. Due to increasing pauperisation leading to loss of land or inadequate growth of productivity on family farms women have withdrawn from active cultivation and thus women cultivators have declined by nearly 50%. On the other hand, number of women agricultural labourers has increased from 12.6 million in 1951 to 15.7 million in 1971 and to 28.83 million in 1991, amounting to one half of the total women force.

The incidence of women agricultural workers is higher in Tamil Nadu than in the country as a whole. The percentage of female agricultural labourers has increased from 11.95 in 1981 to 13.69 in 1991.

According to the international labour review, the work women do on the farm and in the household contributes at least half if not more to the economic development in the country. But of all wrokers, women workers are the most oppressed ones and it is more true about the women working in the agricultural sector, the major unorganised sector of Indian economy. A survey of female agricultural labourers of a few districts in Tamil Nadu provides a profile of the female agricultural labourers.

It is found that around 85% of the female agricultural labourers are illiterate. Majority of them are below poverty line spending less than Rs. 3000 per annum on food. 80% of them are married and a large number of the married women work as labourers due to lack of financial support from their husbands. Most of the agricultural labourers belong to scheduled and most backward communities. The tasks female labourers perform, such as, weeding, and transplanting are considered less strenuous and therefore not equal to the tasks males perform such as ploughing and hence there is wage discrimination between male and female labourers. Most of the labourers are in debt, borrowing money from money lenders at a high rate of interest. They have no other assets besides the few crude implements required for their field work. They have not organised themselves into any union or organisation. The size of an average family of their workers is about five. The younger workers are now in favour of small family norm and desire education for their boys as well as girls. The respondents of the survey have not attended any skill training programmes nor are they aware of any such programmes being conducted for women.

Recommendations

It is necessary to improve the deplorable condition of the female agricultural labourers. Women's access to appropriate technology and systematic training to provide them with necessary skills should be ensured.

Suitable training to involve them in agro based small scale industries and cottage industries should be given so that they can be employed when there is no work on the farm.

Participation of women in Cooperatives and other forms of organisations like Mahila Mandals is necessary so that they have access to welfare services available in health care, nutrition, child care, family planning and literacy programmes.

Rural women should have access to credit and financing.

Women workers should be informed of their legal rights for protection against exploitation. Legal aid centres, legal literacy programmes, lok adalats and family courts would help them become conscious of their rights, especially those regarding minimum wages, equal remuneration, exploitation of child labour, discriminatory treatment of women, etc.

To sum up, women's critical role in agricultural production should be acknowledged and they should receive all key productive inputs, such as credit, modernised equipment and the services of the agricultural extension workers in improving their health, education and quality of life.

PROBLEMS OF WOMEN HEAD LOADERS IN KODAIKANAL

India's forest land cover almost a quarter of its land mass. Forests in the minds of urbanites are either suppliers of industrial raw material or reservoir for diverse flora and fauna. The role of forests in maintaining ecology or in supplying fuelwood, fodder and other life support goods, to the rural poor is a recent realization. The need of the rural people for fuelwood have recently attracted attention. Wood gathering by the poor especially by the rural women is perceived by the elite as an important cause for deforestation.

Kodaikanal Taluk with an area of 21.83 sq. km. is a beautiful hill resort. It has a thick forest area. Wood is the primary fuel for cooking for the natives of Kodaikanal. Most of the women in this area either engage themselves in plantation work or in the collection of fuelwood. A very common sight of any street in Kodaikanal is a woman carrying headload of firewood from the forest. Even from the age of ten, girls are seen carrying fuelwood from the nearby areas. Though the collection and bringing the fuelwood as headload is a strenuous job, it is mostly done by women alone. Generally the men who go for fuelwood bring their collection on horseback.

Objectives of the Study

Since Mother Teresa Women's University aims at the upliftment of women, this study was undertaken to find out the occupational hazards, and other problems faced by the women headloaders in Kodaikanal Taluk. This study was carried out with the following objectives:

1. To find out the socio-economic condition of the women headloaders.

2. To find out the working conditions of these women.
3. To find out the problems they face and to identify their occupational hazards.
4. To find out their role in deforestation.

Methodology

This study was an exploratory cum descriptive one. The data was collected with the help of interview schedule. A pilot study was done to have an empirical evidence regarding structure of the interview schedule, phraseology and so on. Total number of women headloaders in Kodaikanal is around 250 and this number may go up to 400 during season times as reported by the forest officials. By using random sampling method, 100 samples were selected for the study. Opinions from local forest officials and medical officers were also collected.

Major Findings of the Study

1. Women go for wood collection almost every day barring unexpected situations. It was ascertained that a large part of their day is spent in procuring fuelwood.
2. They trek any distance upto 15 miles up and down. The physical strain i.e. exposure to chill climate of Kodaikanal results in headache, body pain, etc.
3. In addition to household chores they put a lot of effort in collecting firewood for their home consumption and for supplementing their family income. The average income per day is around Rs. 20.
4. Most of the women claimed to have started this occupation due to the fact that income from the male folk is inconsistent or insufficient or curtailed due to alcoholism among male members in the family and hence to supplement the family income. Other important reasons for the choice of this occupation are that it is a traditional one and can be plied throughout the year and the stock can also be stored. This is a known occupation which needs no technical skill or investment. Physical effort is the only

input and the reward is in the form of cash that becomes available in a few hours of this operation.

5. They are not exposed to skilled or semiskilled jobs and opportunities for acquiring such skills and employment in such areas are not available in Kodai.

6. Forest officials consider collection of fuelwood from the forest as one of the causes for deforestation. So these wood collectors live constantly in a situation of violating forest rules. The forest officials say that only those women who venture to cut the branches of green trees are questioned and punished. It is also believed that some of these women peel the bark resulting in withering of the trees in course of time. Their role in deforestation is not found to be very significant as they go only for fodder and fuel trees as against well grown timber trees. Hence this may not be a contributing factor for deforestation.

Recommendations to be Implemented

1. In 1982, when late Mr. M.G. Ramachandran, the then Chief Minister of Tamil Nadu visited Kodaikanal, he happened to learn the difficulties of women head loaders. This resulted in some direction to the forest department that the women should not be prevented from taking the discorded woods and dry twigs. This instruction protects the women folk from forest rules to a great extent. This direction given by the Chief Minister needs enactment by amending the existing act as a permanent solution.

2. Every year the forest department takes an overall estimate of the felling trees. These trees are allotted to organizations like South India Viscose, Seshasayee Paper Mart, Tamil Nadu News Print etc. They are allowed to take certain quantity of wood. The remaining wood left out by them is again given for open auction. The woods discorded by these contractors are now being taken by the womenfolk. In this situation, it can be recommended to reserve some felling trees for the natives of Kodaikanal.

3. A nominal fee can be collected at the exit point.

4. Once this occupation is legalised, Co-operative Societies

can be established and arrangements can be made to sell the collection at a reasonable rate.

5. A lorry or some other vehicle can be provided at a minimum fare to carry their collections.
6. Training can be given in such occupations like knitting, weaving, sewing, handicrafts, etc.
7. To reduce cooking drugery and constrain, smokeless chulas can be introduced for the women who collect firewood only for their household purposes.

ENTREPRENEURIAL DEVELOPMENT OF RURAL WOMEN

'The Development of Society requires full participation by all sections of the population and opportunities for full development of the potentialities of women'—this is the key note of the U.N. Declaration on the Elimination of Discrimination against Women.

Unfortunately, provision of opportunities for full development of the potentialities of women remains a pious hope. "While women represent nearly 50% of the adult population and 1/3 of the labour force, they perform nearly 2/3 of all working hours and receive only 1/10th of world income and own less than 1% of the property'.

There is a great difference between men and women in employment pattern, occupation entered, financial returns and unemployment rates. Women are concentrated in low paying dead-end jobs. A study on work participation of men and women reports that where both men and women work full time, year round, the average women worker earns only 3/5th of what a man earns.

According to the census of 1981 of our country, the work participation rate of women in 19.8% as against 52.7% for men. If we look at the distribution of workers by industrial category, about 80% of the women work in the primary sector, as cultivators and agricultural labourers. Only 16% are factory employees. In higher salary brackets, only 2% are women. The level of self employment among women is extremely low as they have very little control on the productive resources and production processes.

The opposition to increasing participation of women springs from the conservative view that women's role should be contained within rigidly defined limits and also from the fear that chronic unemployment may result if women enter the labour market on a large scale. This has resulted in theories of women's marginal role in the economy.

In agrarian societies, the family used to be the unit of production and men, women and children participated in the prodution processes. But transition from traditional agricultural household industries to modern organised industries and services and technological changes in the production methods have affected the role of women in Indian Economy. The general decline of village industries and handicrafts has thrown more and more women on agriculture for their livelihood increasing their numbers and percentage but reducing their levels of employment. In agriculture, role of self employment and wage employment is reversed between male and female workers. Only 29% are cultivators among women, 71% are labourers. Dependence on wage employment has increased during the last decade. Women patta holders in Madurai District is hardly 14%.

A trend analysis at the macro level reveals that women's economic participation has been declining since 1921 both in percentage of workers to total female population and in their percentage of the total labour force. The ratio of female to male workers has declined in all categories and their overall decline in the percentage of women workers is visible in all states for both rural and urban workers, sharper in urban areas.

In Tamil Nadu, the work participation rate is 26.5% for women while that for men is 56.6%. Rural-urban differentials exist in the work participation levels and the urban level is generally lower than the rural and lower for women than men. Only one in nine urban women is working against one in three in rural Tamil Nadu.

Women are greater victims of both unemployment and underemployment. The number of unemployed women in rural areas is about 1 1/2 times as that of unemployed men. Non-workers among female population in TamilNadu is about 74%, 88% in urban and 66% in rural areas.

The basic problems that affect women's role and opportunities for employment spring from their helpless dependence, caused by lack of adequate employment opportunities, limited skills, illiteracy, restricted mobility, and lack of autonomous status. The commercialisation of production and marketing and the rise of intermediaries have caused hardships to a large number of women who were self employed earlier as producers or as retailers.

The declining trend of women's employment in industries is generally attributed to the adverse effects of productive labour laws for women such as maternity benefits, welfare amenities such as creches, separate sanitary facilties, ban on night work and the policy of equalising wages.

Some of the self employment schemes introduced by the social welfare department in training women in cottage industries such as coir making, candle making, palm leaf articles, sericulture etc have not had a significant impact as these activities are very low income generating and therefore not self sustaining.

In the present socio-economic set up, self employment of women requires much more than training in a particular vocation or trade. Self employment will be successful only when women are in a position to market their own products. A programme for generating self employment among women has to be based on an integrated net work of training, production and modern marketing methods and techniques of sales promotion.

If women have to became successful entrepreneurs, the programme should also include training women to develop self confidence, assurance and strength. They should be encouraged to believe in their own ability and develop a sense of self worth.

THE NEW ECONOMIC POLICY AND WOMEN'S DEVELOPMENT

The essentials of the New Economic Policy are liberalisation, deregulation, privatisation, decentralisation, modernisation and globalisation. What possible impact will all these features have on the poor, especially the poor women?

In India, the percentage of rural women to the total female population is 80.5. The average number of working hours per day for a rural woman is 15 to 18, and of this, 8 hours are used for domestic work alone. Almost all the rural women fall below the poverty line. Work of these women includes sowing, weeding, transplanting, harvesting, threshing, winnowing, grass cutting, feeding and milking animals, poultry activities, fetching water, collecting fuel and fodder as well as cook, wash, feed, nurse and look after all the family members. All this work has largely remained invisible to the planners.

The conference report of the United Nations decade for women states that "total development includes development in political, economic, social, cultural and other dimensions of human life as also the physical, intellectual, moral and cultural growth of the human person". Women's development is an essential component in every dimension of development. Involvement and integration of women in development is vital for economic and social success. Thus "development should take care of not only income and employment but also health, education, physical environment, human dignity and freedom". Income generation or economic growth is only a means for development. And again, higher income does not necessarily mean better human development. The USA rates sixth in the work in the scale of per capita income but 44th in its child mortality rate. This is due to uneven distribution of the benefits of economic growth.

In India, during the last 40 years since the planning process started there have been some achievement in some of the priority areas and quite a few failures. Female literacy has risen from 7.6% to 39.1%. Expectation of life at birth is 59 years and adult literacy rate 43%, but this is significantly lower than the average for all developing countries. The average age of marriage has increased to 18.5 for girls. Focus has shifted from welfare to development. There is more involvement of women in the planning and implementation processes at all levels. Efforts have been taken for removing sexist bias and promotion of the value of equality through school curricula. Several legislative enactments and amendments have been passed to protect the interests of women.

As against this rosy picture, we also find that 60% of our women are still illiterate, over 90% of the women work in unorganised sectors where no child care or maternity benefits are available; the number of unemployed girls who have completed school education has risen; 60% of the pregnant women are found to be anaemic; more than one third of the world's poor live in India; more than 400 million people are below poverty line; 75 million children of which 54 million are girls, are not in school; 47 million children under 5 years suffer from malnutrition; 216 million people do not have access to safe drinking water.

In this context how would trade liberalisation, deregulation and decentralisation affect the poor women especially those in the low skill areas such as handloom section, construction activities and small scale industries? What is the experience of the other developing countries?

In Jamaica, deregulation of prices and removal of subsidies led to doubling of food prices which led to a substantial decline in the nutritious standards of children.

In Brazil, wages were pushed down, employment increased, women had to eat less and malnourished women exceeded men in the proportion of 2:1 during the eighties. In Zambia, devaluation of currency led to removal of food subsidies, the price of maize doubled and this caused fierce food rioting and child deaths increased due to malnutrition.

In Sri Lanka, withdrawal of subsidies led to decline of daily per capita calorie consumption.

The per capita income of the average Latin American became 9% lower in 1989 than in 1980. One third of Latin Americans live in dire poverty. Change in nature of employment meant under utilisation of labour force, replacement of full employment by part-time employment and drop in wage income.

In Africa, the number of poor people rose from 210 million to 270 million during the eighties.

The liberalization process in developing countries led to reduce public expenditure on health and education. Withdrawal of food subsidies led to decrease in nutritional standards, increased child mortality rate, increase in child labour, drop in percentage of girls in schools, under employment, drop in real wages etc.

What can be the possible adverse effects of this new policy on women's development in India?

80% of our women are employed in low skills areas and import of modern technology, cheaper imported substitutes for indigeniously manufactured goods would lead to a cut back in the women's jobs. The food factories may take away work home based food processes. Machine print would displace the hand block printers and dyers. Export led growth would divert domestic production to export industries and international competetiveness would lay emphasis on productivity, efficiency and cutting of costs and this may shift the work from men to low paid women. Feminization of labour would increase and non-permanent cheap, contract female labour would be resorted to. Deregulation of labour legislation would increase and protective legislation would be by-passed. Women would be paid less than minimum wages and there would be exploitation by middle men. Unemployment and underemployment among men would increase and there would be drop in real income in the poor families.

The debt crisis may lead to reduce public spending on health and education. Withdrawal of food subsidies would lead to less availability and affordability of food. Child labour would increase and malnutrition among children would lead to increased child mortality rate. Children, especially girls will drop out of schools and lapse into illiteracy; the "Sin and Shame" of illiteracy would continue in the next generation also.

Ela Bhatt, former member of the Planning Commission expresses her anxities and fears when she says that "poor women would become poorer; there would be new poor, borderline poor and chronic poor, there would be more women-headed house holds, there would be more broken families, less work, more migration and more prostitution among women."

Poor women lack transferable skills, knowledge of markets and techniques and access to assets, capital and tools. Hence a credible social safety, security NET should be provided to save women from such possible dangers. The priorities would be to provide universal access to basic education, primary health care for all, provision of safe drinking water, continuation of food subsidies and elimination of malnutrition. There should be programmes for reducing pressures on women's time use. Easy access to safe drinking water, access to fuel and fodder should be provided. They should have greater access to credit. They should be encouraged to participate in marketing; training facilities for women for formation of technical skills and entreprenurial skills should be made available. Price of staple food and fuel should be maintained at affordable level.

It has been proposed that a national renewal fund should be set up for helping those who lose jobs and national work security fund to help in skill upgradation and training of women.

Educational institutions should identify micro issues relating to women, conduct studies and the findings should be used as inputs for macro policy formation.

3

Education and Empowerment of Women

Strategies for empowerment of women

Education and Career training for women

Empowering women in India—New roles for education

Women's studies—an instrument for women's development

General trends in methodology pertaining to women's studies

Development and Advancement of women in management

Women as Agents of transformation in the field of Education

STRATEGIES FOR EMPOWERMENT OF WOMEN

Empowerment is a multi dimensional process which should enable individuals or a group of individuals to realise thier full identity and powers in all spheres of life. It consists of: greater access to knowledge and resources, greater autonomy in decision making to enable them to have greater ability to plan their lives, or have greater control over the circumstances that influence their lives and free them from shackles imposed on them by custom, belief and practice. Generally, development with justice is expected to generate the forces that lead to empowerment of various sections of population in a country and to raise their status.

Discrimination of women from *womb to tomb* is well known. The National perspective plan for women 1988-2000 A.D. (1988) which has made a free, frank, objective and masterly analysis of the impact of developmental plans and programmes of Indian Women, with special reference to Rural Women, gives us the following profile of Women in India.

"There is continued inequality and vulnerability of women in all sectors — economic, social, political, educational, health care, nutrition and legal".

The indicators are as below:-

Women illiterates-	Over 75%
Rural illiterate women	83%
Women, working in unorganised sectors	Over 90%
Of these, unskilled labour in agriculture and construction	83%
Women having full time employment in organised sectors	14%
Maternity benefits and child care available in organised sector	3.5%
Registered unemployed school graduates	51 lakhs
Pregnant women who are anaemic	65%
Infant mortality rate (in the first year of birth)	10%
Of which in slum areas	12.4%
Children dying because of malnutrition before the age of 5 years	40%
Sex ratio— 933 females to every 1000 males	
Expectation of life at birth—51.6 as against 52.6 for males	
property owned by women less than	1%

On an average, a rural woman works for 18 hours a day.

Recent happenings opposed to women's rights to equality and freedom are—renewal of widow immolation.

opposition to a divorced women's right to maintenance, resistence to prohibitions of dowry,

rapid rise of crimes of violence against women—rape, murder, infanticide, foeticide,

Projection of women in the media as sex objects, man eaters or long suffering martyrs accepting humiliation and illtreatment, glamourising their powerlessness

The problems of women are well defined.

What is the cause of her powerlessness? herself? Her nature?

Is she inherently weaker?

Is she a parasite?

Does she naturally need a support?

Is her femaleness the cause of all trouble?

There is a lot of confusion in people's mind regarding nature the inborn traits of women and nurture, the socialisation process that makes here what she becomes.

There is also confusion between sex i.e. (femaleness and maleness) and gender, the role of a male or i.e. female as perceived in society.

The root cause of women's oppression is patriarchy which has snatched legitimate powers from women, making them totally defenceless and powerless. Hence woman need to be empowered not as a favour to them but for undoing the injustice meted out to them.

Soviet President, Mikhail Gorbachev, in his welcome address to the World Congress of Women at Moscow in June 1987 said, "The Status of Women is a barometer of the democratism of any State, an indicator of how human rights are respected in it."

As women are oppressed in all spheres of life, they need to be empowered in all walks of life. There cannot be a piecemeal approach to women's empowerment. Hence all aspects of society have to be restructured.

Empowerment is an active process. Power is not a commodity to be transacted. Power cannot be given away as alms. Power has to be acquired. Once acquired, it needs to be exercised, sustained and preserved. Women have to empower themselves.

Governments may offer welfare schemes for women. They may float anti-poverty programmes. They may launch projects for their uplift. They may enact legislation to safeguard women's rights. The Government policies can only facilitate the process, reduce the hurdles and create an atmosphere conducive to transformation. But it is the women who have to empower themselves. Unless they themselves become conscious of their oppression, show initiative and seize the opportunities, it would not be possible to change their status.

Pandit Jawaharlal Nehru once said-"To awaken the people, it is women who must be awakened; once she is on the move, the family moves, the village moves and the nation moves."

The empowerment mechanism is easily enumerated. But the question is the operationalisation. We all agree that women should have :

higher literacy and education

better care of health for herself and her children

higher age at marriage

acceptance of a small family norm

greater work participation in modernised sector

self reliance, self respect and dignity among women

better consciousness of their rights

no dependence on males

higher standard of living etc.

How do we operationalize all these?

What should be the role of Universities and Colleges in empowerment?

What is our social commitment?

Let us empower our own students, first, by

- removing sex bias in our curriculum and by designing courses incorporating women's dimensions
- emphasising on the multiple role of women
- developing the ability to think creatively about situations the hurdles to face, possibilities of change, the coping mechanism etc.

- overcoming social taboos and traditional beliefs
- encouraging late marriages
- sensitizing them to laws related to property, marriage, divorce, minimum wages, maternity leave benefit etc.
- encouraging them to take careers seriously
- encouraging to believe in their own ability and a sense self worth
- helping them to develop interest in application of science
- making them aware of possibilities of self employment
- educating parents on the importance of making women economically self sufficient

Let us, through our extension activities, get our students to take up action programmes to raise the consciousness of rural women and empower them.

Development tasks connected with health care, environmental safety, promotion of population, education activities, family welfare, citizenship roles and responsibilities, legal rights, drudgery reduction, combating atrocities and violences committed to women, etc. could be taken up in our community service, social service and adult education activities.

EDUCATION AND CAREER TRAINING FOR WOMEN

Equality between men and women in Education

Historical Perspective

The most noteworthy feature of ancient Indian Education is the Education of Women. Women were given equal rights with men in all ways of life, including education. Ladies have been quoted as *authors* of some of the Samhitas of Rig Veda. We hear of lady *Philosophers* and of *Brahma Vadinis* who dedicated their whole lives to education. We find that women had the freedom to remain single as well as freedom to choose their life partners. We have ample evidence to prove that *Co-education* existed in the Ashrams. But as conditions changed, *when girls started to lose the privileges of education, the marriage age came down, they lost their equality, came to be considered as mere possessions* and by 100 A.D. i.e. Manu's time, they were ascribed completely to dependant status. This law giver has said, "By a girl, by a young women, or even by an aged, nothing must be done independently even in her own home". During the middle ages, seclusion or "Pardah" was added to the existing subordinate and subservient status of women and in course of time, women became completely illiterate and entirely dependent on men—father, husband and son, economically, socially and culturally.

All over the world, the movement for improving women's status has always emphasised education as the most significant instrument for social change. The social reformers of the 19th centruy tried to use education more to ameliorate the position of women socially; they were able to awaken the consciousness of the nation to the evils of child marriage, sati, polygamy, enforced widowhood, dowry system, etc. Since the new western education which developed during the 19th century invariably meant "a method of earning" and since women were not required to earn, it was not considered necessary for women to be educated. Learning to do household work was sufficient for her and so the parents were not keen to incur any expenditure in educating the girls till very recently.

Progress since Independence

Literacy

During the present century, the country has made spectacular progress in promoting the interests of women. The literacy rate went up from about 7% in 1901 to 7.9% in 1951, 18% in 1971 and 24.88% in 1981. But there is still a wide gap between male and female literacy . This is obvious from the following table:

Literacy Rate in India

	1951	*1961*	*1971*	*1981*	*1991*
Male	24.9%	34.4%	39.51%	46.74%	63.86%
Female	7.9%	12.9%	18.44%	24.88%	39.43%
Total	16.6%	24.0%	29.45%	36.0%	52.11%

This disparity between men's and women's participation in education becomes greater at the more advanced levels of education.

Eventually, the intake of females in technical and higher education is considerably low. But it is heartening to see that women are enrolled in all vocational and professional courses, namely polytechnics, medicine, teaching, veterinary, engineering, physical education, agriculture, law and fine arts. There are about 475 research institutions for women.

Full integration of women in Development

Education for National Development

Education was for long dissociated from the idea of nation building. It was viewed as a process for infusing piety, during the ancient period. It was then seen as a cultural process, to transmit the accumulated wealth of knowledge, to impart classical values, and to build character of the individual. It was essentially for a privileged few and hence was not really contributory to the development of the nation as we understand today. When the demand for women's education started in the 18th century, it was more in the light of women's rights, for the access to knowledge and not *as a national economic asset.* Then the attitude has changed and for the first time, the UNESCO conference in 1962 underlined the importance of the access of girls and women to technical and vocational education for economic and social development.

According to Gunar Myrdal (1969), education has an "independent" as well "instrumental" value, i.e. the purpose of education must be to rationalize attitudes as well as to impart knowledge and skills. Education for national development should include education for self reliance, personal development, social development, productive capacity, social integration and political understanding.

Do we educate our girls for such an integrated development? What type of education should we plan? What type of curriculum should we develop to train the intellect, to discipline the emotions for social advancement and for creative contribution of our girls? Is it enough to merely train her for her future careers as wife and mother? Shall we continue the present system where the girls are educated to desperately complete with men in all odd professions? Or should we educate her according to her aptitude and ability and help her to attain the fullest possible development in all respects, personally, socially and economically and thus live a complete life?

Harnessing Women Power

Rationale

The Indian constitution has guranteed "Equal rights and equal opportunities to all its citizens, irrespective of sex, age, race or religion." The rights are guaranteed by law, but yet to be legalized in custom.

The International conference on public education convened jointly by UNESCO and the Inteernational Bureau of Education in Geneva 1952, while discussing the question of access of women to education, made the following recommendations to ministries of education of all member countries.

1. Every person without distinction of sex should enjoy all the rights and freedom proclaimed by the universal "Declaration of Human Rights", and that such equality should apply in all fields, particularly that of education.
2. Every person, man or woman should be able to receive an education enabling him to develop his aptitudes as fully as possible, playing an effective part as member or citizen of his community, his nation and the world and meet the demands of his special tasks in life.
3. Women, like men, should have opportunities to fulfil the tasks appropriate to their aptitudes.
4. General education should be equal in value and status to that of boys and thus avoid social discrimination.

With the recognition of women as human beings having equal rights with men, has risen the parallel concept of equality of contribution to public and private life.

The constitution has granted social and political equality; perhaps India is the first country which decided on adult suffrage at the start of a parliamentary democracy and gave the rights to women at the same time as men. Political franchise extended to women would become meaningless if they are not able to understand the issues their votes are to decide. Social equality are practised by millions of women who have come out of their seclusion; a few pockets of orthodoxy still continues to react.

In the sphere of economic activity very few women have developed the ability to stand on their own feet and be completely independent. Majority of women follow merely the profession of matrimony and they remain dependent on men. Women have to be trained for economic emancipation. The participation of women in social, economic, political, and cultural life would decide the country's advancement and success.

Career Training for Women

All over the world, education is being reshaped for the following reasons:

More and more linkages are being developed between education and work; there is a great concern for the rising rates of youth unemployment. There is a great need to create labour force which would be capable of work in the growing complexity of technological application; proper attitudes and skills for employability have to be developed among the youth; there is a shift in proportion of women leaving the home and entering the work force. All these point to the need for an adequate programme of career guidance for the school learners.

In India, since independence, i.e. 1947, provision of educational opportunities to women has been an important programme in the educational sector. Between 1951 and 1981, through the percentages of literacy among women has improved from 7.83% to 24.82% women still comprise 57% of the illiterate population and 70% of the non-enrolled children of the school stage are girls. In spite of the efforts made so far, the educational system has not been able to make sufficient contribution towards women's equality.

One of the targets of the New Policy on Education is that there should be increased women's access to vocational, technical, professional education and to existing an emergent technologies. The Action Programme of the NPE recommends that the choice of trades and disciplines offered to women at all levels in all types of technical education institutions should be made in keeping with the view the objective of bringing about women's equality. The NPE also says that identification of certain skills and occupations as 'suitable' or 'relevant' for women should no longer dictate the choice of subject in the education institutions. The selection of subject should be based on the employment potential; counselling services should be provided to enable to opt for the new subejct and courses in the emerging technologies and programmes.

"While women represent nearly 50% of the adult population, and 1/3 of the labour force, they perform nearly 2/3 of all working hours and receive only 1/10th of the world income and own less than 1% of the property".

Very few women happen to be in a position to influence political thinking or the decision making process. In the union cabinet, there is hardly one woman minister to every 5 men. With a low level of participation in the decision making process at the government level, their impact on the political process and decision making is not significant.

There is a great difference between men and women in employment pattern, occupation entered, financial returns and unemployment rates. Women are concentrated in low paid dead-end jobs. One of the research findings is that where both men and women work full time, year round, the average woman worker earns only about 3/5th what a man earns. To achieve equality with the males, a great percentage of women would have to change occupations and take up new careers.

According to the census of 1981, in India the work participation rate of women is 19.8% as against 52.7% for men. If we look at the distribution of workers by industrial category, about 80% of the women are agricultural labourers and cultivators. Factory employees are only 16%. Even in the administrative service as IAS where there is no sex discrimination, hardly 12% are women. In higher salary brackets, 2% are women. Level of self employment among women is extremely low as they have very little control among production processes.

Among the students joining Engineering Colleges, only 7% are girls, and hardly 1% choose special courses as chemical technology, printing technology, textile technology etc. Among the students joining polytechnics, 17% are girls. The entrants to law college is in the ratio 1 : 5. Among doctors, 24% are women whereas 97% of the nurses are girls. Among the students who join pharmacy, 28% are girls, in the veterinary service, hardly 8% of the girls join.

Though the status of women's educational attainment has generally improved, with 40% girls finishing high school level, 45% completing Higher Secondary, 40% joining colleges, 47% joining medical colleges etc, women are still under represented in business management, engineering, physical science, professional courses such as dentistry, optometry, pharmacy, law etc. Girls still hesitate to enter non-traditional courses such as Computer Science, Photography, Aerospace Engineering, Accountancy, Administration, Research in Sciences etc.

The most serious omission in conceptualizing career choice is the consideration of the effects of sex role socialisation on the decision making process. Career choice and career decisions are influenced by the decisions about marriage, parenthood, female-male responsibilities in home making etc. Social norms and expected sex roles also have an impact on the career decisions. Women are not really free to explore their interest and make choices with a more consicous perspective. Girls' capabilities are underestimated by the parents, teachers and the society. Usually, girls are not able to battle on their own, give way to pressure and thus we find a vast array of women occupying low paid posts as stenos, typists, nurses, factory workers, sales girls, primary schools teachers etc. Again in a conservative society like ours, aiming high in the external world of success and power by women is not relished. In an achieving society, men cannot offord to fail and women need not succeed. Men have a right to aim high and they are always in danger of being despised if they do not move upwards - but not so with women. Usually girls are not taken seriously as careerists as it is considered to be of secondary importance. Marriage is the principal determinant of a woman's social position and it is more important to get married to men with high paid jobs. The loss is to the nation, of the work the girls could do and the tremendous disappointment for girls who do not find a rewarding career. Girls who might have been successful architects, lawyers or engineers end up in safe jobs as teachers or nurses.

The traditional myths about work which still continue to influence the career of women are:

1. Husbands will support and the girls do not need to work.
2. Girls do not need well paid jobs like men because they do not have to support their families. They work only for pin-money.
3. Women's work is in the home. Those who work outside neglect their homes and children.
4. All women have to get married and will stay married .

5. The men they marry will never become unemployed or incapacitated and will always support their families.
6. Married women and mothers are not reliable workers.
7. Women may work until they marry.

Sex role stereotyping influences our lives from birth and is a powerful influence in schools. This results in restrictions upon the freedom of occupational choice and career development for boys and girls.

If girls' careers are to be taken seriously, the significance of subjects like Science and Maths should be explained to them even when they are about 13 to 14 years. If women have to be appointed to positions of authority, guidance should be given to them in school stage itself for developing self-confidence, assurance and strength. They have got to learn to be assertive, firm and dynamic. Girls should be exposed to a few models of women occupying superior roles.

Teachers, especially women teachers, should give extra encouragement to girls both to believe in their own ability and a sense of self worth, so that they will go for top careers.

The message that a girl can, if she has the will to do so, earn as much as her husband, do as interesting a job and take her work as seriously as he does, has to be passed on.

EMPOWERING WOMEN IN INDIA—NEW ROLES FOR EDUCATION

Women and Education

Historical Perspective: Where Women were

The most noteworthy feature of ancient Indian Education is the education of women. Women were given equal rights with men in all walks of life, including education. Ladies have been quoted as authors of some of the samhitas of Rig Veda. We hear of lady philosophers and Brahma Vadinis who dedicated their whole lives to education. We find that women had the freedom to remain single as well as freedom to choose their life partners. We have ample evidence to prove that co-education existed in the Ashrmas. But as conditions changed, when girls started to lose the privileges of education, the marriage age came down, they lost their equality, came to be considered as mere possessions and by 100 A.D. i.e. Manu's time, they were ascribed completely to a dependent status. This law giver has said, "By a girl, by a young woman, or even by an aged, nothing must be done independantly even in her own home". During the middle ages, seclusion or "Pardah" was added to the existing subordinate and subservient status of women and in course of time, women became completely illiterate and entirely dependant on men—father, husband and son, economically, socially and culturally.

All over the world, the movement for improving women's status has always emphasised education as the most significant instrument for social change. The social reformers of the 19th Century tried to use education more to ameliorate the position of women socially; they were able to awaken the consciousness of the nation to the evils of child marriage, sati, polygamy, enforced widowhood, dowry system etc. Since the new western education which developed during the 19th Centruy invariably meant "a method of earning" and since women were not required to earn, it was not considered necessary for women to be educated. Learning to do household work was sufficient for her and so the parents were not keen to incur any expenditure in educating the girls till very recently.

Where Women Are—A Situational Analysis: Progress Since Independence

Literacy

During the present century, the country has made spectacular progress in promoting the interests of women. The literacy rate went up from about 7% in 1901 to 7.9% iin 1951. 18% in 1971. 24.88% in 1981 and 39.63% in 1991. But there is still a wide gap between male and female literacy. This is obvious from the following table:

Literacy Rate in India

	1951	*1961*	*1971*	*1981*	*1991*
Male	24.9%	34.4%	39.51%	46.74%	63.86%
Female	7.9%	12.9%	18.44%	24.88%	39.43%
Total	16.6%	24.0%	29.45%	36.00%	52.11%

Among the males, the corresponding rise is from 24.9% to 46.7% i.e. the gap in percentage literacy points between male and female literacy has increased from 17 in 1951 to 22 in 1981. In absolute terms too, the number of illiterate women has increased during this period from 158.7 million to 241.7 million in 1981 and to 352 million in 1991. Women comprised 57% of the illiterate population in 1981 and 45% in 1991; girls formed 70% of non-enrolled children in 1981, 60% in 1991 in the school age group. Three fourths of the 50 million children who are not enrolled in any school are girls. It is estimated that 30% of the total work of fuel gathering, fetching water and farm work is done by girls between 6 and 11 years. Almost the entire burden of sibling care is on the girl child.

Enrolment of Boys and Girls in School—A Comparative Picture

In 1951, enrolment of boys in the primary stage was 55% of the population in the corresponding age group and among girls, enrolment was only 20.1%

At the middle stage, 4.6% girls enrolled as against 20.8% of boys.

At the secondary stage, for every 100 boys, only 16 girls enrolled. Enrolment of women in university education was about 11 for every 100 men.

In 1981, for every 100 boys, the number of girls enrolled in the primary stage is 64, middle stage is 51, secondary stage is 31, university stage is 30 and vocational, technical education is 20. The male-female gaps have narrowed to a certain extent but girls are behind in numbers and the type of education.

In 1991, 42% of the pupils enrolled at primary school are girls and only 33% are enrolled in secondary school.

Though the number of schools has increased phenomenally, in classes I to V, (age group 6-11 years) one out of every three girls is still outside the school. The dropout rates for girls is very high, one out of every three girls is still outside the school. Of every 100 girls in Class I, only 30 reach Class V. In Classes VI-VIII (age group 11-14 years) only 27 out of every 100 girls are at school as compared to 54 boys in this age group. At the secondary stage: i.e. Classes IX to XII, (in the age group 14-17 years) only 20 out of every hundred girls are in school as against 39 boys. Girls form less than one third of the total enrolment at the secondary level.

According to 1991 figures, of every 100 girls in Class I, 73 remain in Class II, 45 enter Class V and only 4 end up in Class XII.

Girls' position is worse in vocational, professional and other special schools at the secondary level. Girls go in only for female sex-typed courses such as nursing, teacher training, home science, music etc. and very few girls enrol in technical courses leading to industry.

Female enrolment in higher education has gone up more than thirty points since 1951, the proportion of women to every hundred men at the University stage has increased from 14 to 46 in the past 36 years. But a large number of girls opt for general Arts and Humanities courses. In 1981, of every 100 girls enrolled, 56 were in Arts, 21 in Science, 13 in Commerce, 7 in Engineering and 3.6 in Medicine. The number of women, per 100 men, faculty wise, was 60.5 in Arts, 40.4 in Science, 19.2 in Commerce, 91.9 in Education, 4 in Engineering and Technical Education, 32.5 in Medicine, 2.6 in Agriculture and 7.4 in Law. By 1987, enrolment of girls in Engineering increased by three times and in Medicine, one and a half times.

There is uneven rate of progress of all levels of education not only between states but between different levels of education in the same state. There is vast disparity between education of girls in rural areas and urban areas. Therer is a big gap between enrolment of girls belonging to the scheduled caste/tribe and other castes. Girls belonging to scheduled caste and tribes are also lagging behind boys belonging to SC/ST.

Labour Force participation of Women in India

The pattern of women's participation in the labour force can indicate women's education in preparing them for participation in national development on equal terms with men.

We find the work participation rate of women is low in India, has declined from 33.7% in 1911 to 20.85% in 1981 the corresponding rate of male work participation in 1981 being 52.7%

If we look at the distribution of workers by individual category, 80% of the women workers are engaged in agriculture, 13% in organised sector of the economy and the rest in unorganised non-agricultural occupations. Of these women workers, more then 89% are illiterate, about 50% of the total 'non working' women are engaged in household activities, hardly 0.2% are women of independent means. Even in the administrative services like IAS, IFS, where there is no sex discrimination, hardly 7.5% are women. In 1988, there were 339 women IAS officers, out of a total of 4548. The Indian Forest Service has only 10 women officers i.e. 0.6% and in the IPS, there were 21 women officers as against 2418 men. The proportion of seats won by women to the Lok Sabha was 46 out of 537 seats. The Rajya Sabha had 28 women in a home of 245 seats. The pattern is similar at the State level. The incidence of unemployment also is high in that, they account for 40% of the total unemployment, which is higher than their share in the labour force which is 33%. The wage differentials between men and women continue to exist in spite of legislation enacted for "equal pay for equal work". It is also found that women are predominantly employed in consumption linked services and not in production linked industrial occupations. Female workers are concentrated in unskilled, low status, low prestige, dead end jobs such as midwives, health visitors, clerks, teachers, unskilled office workers, food preservers, canners, nurses etc. Thus we can see that women are hurdled at the lowest occupational structure of the modern sector and the males continue to dominate the top echelons.

Studies also show that mechanisation and modernisation have marginalised women in many sectors. They are being pushed down or out of the work force.

The average hours of unpaid work done by women outside their homes in rural areas vary from 6 to 7 hours a day. But their access to ownership of land and other productive resources remains negligible.

30 to 35% of the rural household are headed by women due to male migration or abandonment.

Women comprise only 7.5% of the membership of registered trade unions, hardly one per cent being office bearers. Representation of women in elected offices has remained stagnant, in spite of the increased voting turn out in general election.

Other Indication of Women's Status

Age specific death rates indicate higher rates for female child. The fertility rate has not declined to the desired extent, the average number of children born to a woman in her lifetime being 4.6. More than half of the women do not get sufficient dietary intake of calories, proteins, calcium, iron, vitamin A. Two thirds of the pregnant women are anaemic, crimes against women continue unabated. There is resistance to prohibition of dowry. The projection of women in the media as sex objects, man eaters, or long suffering martyrs, accepting humiliation and illtreatment glamourize their powerlessness.

Some postitive indices are :

The expectation of life at birth was 52.9% years in 1981 and it has risen from 44.7 years in 1961. In 1991 it has risen to 55.9 years, equal to that of man.

The sex ratio has registered a slight increase, from 930 women per 1000 males in 1971 to 933 in 1981. But in 1991 it has come down to 927 females for every 1000 males.

The average age at marriage has reached 18.3 years in 1981 as against 17.1 in 1971.

The focus in the programmes for women has shifted from welfare to development and empowerment.

Where women might Be:

What is the cause of her powerlessness?

Herself or her nature?

Is she inherently weaker?

Is she a parasite?

Does she naturally need a support?

Is her femaleness the cause of all trouble?

There is a lot of confusion in people's mind regarding nature i.e. the inborn traits of women and nurture, i.e., the socialisation process that makes her what she is. There is also confusion between sex i.e. femaleness and maleness and gender i.e. the role of a male or female as perceived in the society.

The root cause of women's oppression is patriarchy, which has snatched legitimate powers from women, making them totally defenceless and powerless. Hence women need to be empowered for undoing the injustice meted out to them.

Empowerment Process

Empowerment is an active, multi-dimensional process which should enable women to realise their full indentity and powers in all spheres of life. It would consist of greater access to knowledge and resources, greater autonomy in decision making, greater ability to plan their lives, have greater control over the circumstances that influence their lives and free them from shackles imposed on them by custom, belief and practice. Generally, development with justice is expected to generate the forces that lead to empowerment of various sections of population in a country and to raise their status.

But, power is not a commodity to be transacted. Power cannot be given away as alms. Power has to be acquired and once acquired, it needs to be exercised, sustained and preserved. Women have to empower themselves. Unless they themselves become conscious of their oppression, show initiative and seize the opportunities, it would not be possible to change their status.

The empowerment mechanism is easily enumerated

higher literacy and education

better health care for herself and her children

higher age at marriage

greater work participation in modernized sector

necessary financial and service support

advancement into higher position of power

better consciousness of their rights

self reliance, self respect and dignity among women

What is the role of education in the process of empowerment? How do we operationalise these concepts?

How Education Can be used for Empowering Women

Education for National Development

Education was for long disassociated from the idea of nation building. It was viewed as a process for infusing piety, during the ancient period. It was then seen as a cultural process, to transmit the accumulated wealth of knowledge, to impart classical values, and to build character of the individual. It was essentially for a privileged few and hence was not really contributory to the development of the nation as we understand today. When the demand for women's education started in the 18th centruy, it was more in the light of women's rights, for the access to knowledge and not as a national economic asset. Then the attitude changed and for the first time, the UNESCO Conference in 1962 underlined the importance of the access of girls and women to technical and vocational education for economic and social development.

According to Gunnar Myrdal (1969), education has an independent as well "instrumental" value, i.e. the purpose of education must be to rationalise attitude as well as to impart knowledge and skills. Education for national development should include education for self reliance, personal development, scoial development, productive capacity, social integration and political understanding.

Do we educate our girls for such an integrated development? What type of education should we plan? What type of curriculum should we develop to train the intellect, to discipline the emotions for social advancement and for creative contribution of our girls? Is it enough to merely train her for her future career as wife and mother? Shall we continue the present system where the girls are educated merely to obtain a degree which is a passport to matrimony? Or, should we educate her according to her aptitude and ability and help her to attain the fullest possible development in all respects, personally, socially and economically and thus lead a complete life?

Harnessing Women Power: Rationale

The Indian constitution has guarateed "Equal rights and equal opportunities to all its citizens, irrespective of sex, age, race or religion". The rights are guaranteed by law, but yet to be legalized in custom.

The International Conference on public education convened jointly by UNESCO and the International Bureau of Education, in Geneva 1952, while discussing the question of access of women to education, made the following recommendations to ministries of education of all member countries.

1. Every person, without distinction of sex should enjoy all the rights and freedom proclaimed by the "Universal Declaration of Human Rights", and that such equality should apply in all fields, particularly that of education.

2. Every person, man or woman should be able to receive an education enabling him to develop his aptitude as fully as possible, playing an effective part as member or citizen of his community, his nation and the world and meet the demands of his special tasks in life.

3. Women, like men, should have opportunities to fulfil the tasks appropriate to the aptitudes.

4. General education should be equal in value and status of that of boys and thus avoid social discrimination.

With the recognition of women as human beings having equal rights with men, has risen the parallel concept of equality of contribution of public and private life.

The constitution has granted social and political equality; perhaps India is the first country which decided on adult suffrage at the start of a parliamentary democracy and gave the rights to women at the same time as men. Political franchise extended to women would become meaningless if they are not able to understand the issues their votes are to decide. Social equality is practised by millions of women who have come out of their seclusion, a few pockets of orthodoxy still continues to react.

In the sphere of economic activity very few women have developed the ability to stand on their own feet and be completely independent. majority of women follow merely the profession of matrimony and remain dependent on men. Women have to be trained for economic emancipation. The participation of women in social, economic, political and cultural life would decide the country's advancement and success.

Career Training for Women

All over the world, education is being reshaped for the following reasons.

More and more linkages are being developed between education and work; there is a great concern for the rising rates of youth unemployment. There is a great need to create a labour force which would be capable of working in the growing complexity of technological application; proper attitudes and skills for employability have to be developed among the youth; there is a shift in proportion of women leaving the home and entering the work force. All these points to the need for an adequate programme of career guidance for the school leavers.

There should be increased access for women to vocational, technical and professional education and to the existing and emergent technologies. The choice of disciplines offered to women at all levels in all types of technical education should be in keeping with the objective of bringing about women's equality. The identification of some skills and occupation as "suitable" or "relevant" to women should no longer dictate the choice of subjects. The selection of subject should be based on the aptitude of the individual and the employment potential. Adequate counselling services should be made available to all the students.

The most serious omission in conceptualizing career choice is the consideration of the effects of sex role socialisation on the decision making process. Career choices and career decisions are influenced by the decisions about marriage, parenthood, female-male responsibilities in home making etc. Social norms and expected sex roles also have an impact on career decision. Women are really not free to emplore their interest and make choices with a more conscious perspective. Girls' capabilities are usually under estimated by the parents, teachers and the society. Indian girls have not been trained adequately by the educational institutions to be able to battle on their own and hence they give way to pressure and thus we find a vast number of able women ending up in low status, low paid jobs. Again, in a conservative society like India, aiming high in the external world of suceess and power by women is not relished. Usually, girls are not taken seriously as carrists as career is considered to be of secondary importance. Marriage is the principal determinant of a women's social position and it is more important to get married to men with high paid jobs.The traditional myth such as—girls do not need to work, the husband's duty is to support them, women's work is in the house, and those who work outside neglect thier homes and children; women may work until they marry; married women and mothers are not reliable workers; women are poor at qualitative analysis and unable to make tough decisions etc.—continue to influence women's career and act as barrier to women's advancement into senior positions.

If girls' careers are to be taken seriously the significance of subjects like Science and Mathematics should be explained to them in the middle school itself. Guidance should be given to them at the school stage itself for developing self confidence, assurance and strength, They have got to learn to be assertive, firm and dynamic. Teachers should give extra encouragement to girls both to believe in their own ability and sense of self worth. Education should help in training of skills such as overcoming fear of failure, coping with stress, developing resistance to criticism and willingness to take risks.

Curricula and textbooks should be redesigned to include values and process commensurate with the new status of women.

Values identified are:

1. Home management, a joint responsibility of all members
2. respect for the roles performed inside and outside the home
3. equal participation in the development of the nation
4. equal commitment for work at home and outside by both the sexes
5. decision making process at all levels to be shared by both the sexes
6. women not to be projected as sex symbols or prosperity symbols
7. no dependance syndrome but women to be self reliant, self propelled and self directed
8. no degrading of women in matrimony such as bride price, dowry, sati etc.
9. development of vocational skills and competencies for economic independence.

Empowerment of rural women should be the priority area of non-formal, adult and continuing education programmes. Stress on need based functional education and skill development in the practical utility areas would attract enrolment of girls in non-formal education. People in mass media, folk media, functionaries of voluntary agencies, performing artists and creative workers should be sensitized to promote the indentified values of empowerment of women.

References

1. Bhatia S.C. Education and Social Cultural Disadvance, Delhi Xeres Publication, 1982.
2. Chattopadhyay, Kamala Devi, Indian Women's Battle for Freedom, New Delhi, Abhinav Publications, 1983.
3. Ghadially, Rehana (Ed) Women in Indian Society, New Delhi. Sage Publication, 1988.
4. Hughes, Mary and Kennedy, Mary,' New Futures: Changing Women's Education, Routledge and Kegan Paul, 1985.
5. Pillai. J.K. Readings in Women's Education, Kodaikanal, Mother Teresa Women's University, 1988.
6. Slipman, Sue. Helping ourselves to power, Oxford. Pergamon Press, 1986.
7. Towards Equality: Report of the committee on the Status of Women in India, Government of India, Department of Social Welfare, Ministry of Education and Social Welfare, New Delhi, December 1974.
8. National Perspective Plan for Women (1988-2000 A.D.) Report of the Core group set up by the Department of Women and Child Development, Ministry of Human Resources Development, Government of India, 1988.

WOMEN'S STUDIES—AN INSTRUMENT FOR WOMEN'S DEVELOPMENT

Definition

Women's Studies is variously defined as -

"Studying women with a women's Perspective"

"Looking at women from women's point of view"

"A balanced understanding of women's reality"

"A critical understanding of women's contribution to the social processes" etc.

"The process of becoming aware of the oppression and

discrimination to which women have been subjected and using this as a power to change the situation" has evolved into women's studies. The main force behind women's studies is the movement to assert the interests of women as a sex. It does not mean women wanting to be men or women wanting to dominate men but it is a demand to restore to half of humanity its rightful place in society, to restore to women their humanity".

Functions

The function of Women's Studies, according to Vina Mazumdar is "to discover, acquire and accumulate knowledge about women, so that all of us, not just women, can perhaps start looking at human beings and societies in a different way". The commitment of women's studies is to improve the status and position of women.

A student of women's studies has an interest in a number of disciplines. She does not conceive of knowledge in a compartmentalised way. Women's studies is essentially interdisciplinary, i.e, it integrates disciplinary perspectives. It is also transdisciplinary as it goes beyond the disciplines. Women's studies is a move away from the narrow disciplinary specialisations and their jargons. It tries to discover a common language, a simple language that all can understand. It tries to correct the inadequacies of traditional desciplines - History that ignores women's contribution, Economics that ignores women's work at home and the farm and brands this work as 'non productive labour', Education that fails to address itself to educating girls to promote equality, Sociology which does not question the discrimination and oppression of women in society, Psychology that ignores the strenghts of women, and Law that reveals a bias against women—which are distorted disciplines.

The strategies used by women's studies are threefold—research, teaching and action.

Research

Why?

1. Very little is known about the large majority of women who are invisible and whose contribution to development is considerable. Reliable information is needed for policy making.

2. We need to dispel myths, prejudices, beliefs and practices which do not treat men and women as equals. This is necessary for raising women's self esteem which is so necessary for helping them to help themselves.

3. Research is also necessary for building up materials of teaching, training and awareness. A substantial body of knowledge is most imminent for a better understanding of issues.

Research in Women's Studies should centre around problems—Social and Political. The traditional methodology of social sciences, such as statistical survey of a huge sample, and participant observation should be substituted by non- conventional techniques such as conscientisation, interventionist, participatory and experiential analysis, which take into account the experiences of both the researcher and the researched. This naturally requires a small size of sample and the style of writing the report should eschew statistical jargons. It should be story like telling of the findings - a simple language which all can understand. Women's studies scholars should not be obsessed with method per se but the problem to be studied should determine the method to be used. The choice of the problem is also crucial. Questions which are real to the members of the women's community should be the concern of Women's Studies. Research in Women's studies should not become just another piece of research as in most social sciences, removed from the daily world, and hence gathering dust in the libraries of the universities. Research in Women's Studies should generate new knowledge through exhaustive field study and this knowledge should deepen the base of various disciplines and used for correction of development policies and programmes.

Action

Women's Studies can not remain as an ivory tower discipline but has to study and change the following:

- 80% of women are illiterate
- 70% of the drop-outs are girls
- Only 60% of the girls in the age group 6-11 are actually enrolled in schools
- sexist bias in all curricula—School and College

- gender discrimination in the bringing up of children
- declining sex ratio - (927 females for every 1000 males) due to female infanticide, female foeticide, bride burning etc.
- increasing female poverty
- lower life expectancy of women
- atrocities and violence against women
- domination of patriarchy
- only a decimal percentage of girls join higher education
- curriculum of higher education ignores women's dimensions
- invisibility of women in History, Political Science and Social Sciences.

Teaching

The male perceptions throughout our modern disciplines is overriding. Theories have been derived from, based on, and reinforce the experiences, beliefs and perception of men only. The fallacy about women has been that "women is not only unknown but unknowable". This has to be corrected. The main task of women's studies is to make women visible in the curriculum. There is universal undervaluation of women and their work. Women's Studies has to start with the premise that gender discrimination does prevail in society and that women are considered inferior. The experiences at the field level should be brought into the class room. Women's studies should not be taught through conventional class room methods but non-traditional, experiential, participatory methods should be used to make our students sensitive to the issues.

Conclusion

Women's Studies should be compulsory at the undergraduate level, open to both boys and girls. It should have a contemporary approach and be topical, including the burning issues of today.

> "It is high time to examine the life of women as human beings in the context of their actual lives, hopes, aspirations and expectations and to take steps to change the self effacing, submissive and inferior role of women today".

GENERAL TRENDS IN METHODOLOGY PERTAINING TO WOMEN'S STUDIES

Women's studies is a newly emerging discipline in the social sciences. The main function of women's studies is to discover, acquire and to accumulate knowledge about women, with the specific focus on women as an analytical category. Underlying the focus is the recognition "that 'women are frequently a specially oppressed group within each unit of social economic structural pattern, whether it is caste, class or race".

The International Women's Year, 1975, gave a great impetus to studies with a specific focus on women's lives all over the world, including India. In the last ten years, a fair number of studies on a diversity of themes, using many methodology and integrating many disciplines have been done.

It would be apt to review the trend of the studies undertaken to see the trends in methodology. Women's studies in India is not just ten years old. During the 19th Centruy, when the social reform movement highlighted the many forms of women's oppression, such as sati, child marriage, polygamy etc., enquiries on women's role in the family, marriage, kinship, network etc., were undertaken. But there were essentially descriptive macro studies attempted by Indologists, Anthropologists and Social Historians.

During the thirties and forties of this century, the participation of women in the struggle for freedom led to changing perceptions regarding women's role and the focus of the enquiries shifted to women's participation in national development—economic, social and political.

During the sixties the dual role of women became an important area of study. Women's level of education and its relationship to development give birth to correlational studies on Women's educational status and its relationship to population, birth rate, poverty, malnutrition etc. Some of them were micro studies, analytical, problem focussed and with a thrust on hypothesis testing. Analysis on demographic information, educational levels of occupational distribution etc., were provided by these studies. Thus the shift was from Macro to Micro, general to particular and from documentary analysis to participatory observation using in depth interviews and questionnaire techniques.

The Report of the Committee on the Status of Women in India (Government of India, 1975) provided a data base and highlighted the various priority areas regarding women which needed to be studied.

Women's oppression and subordination is one area which has been studied all over the world, during the last 10-15 years. These studies have given an understanding of women's secondary status and its linkage with the economic and political structure of the respective countries as well as the influence of cultural traditions and religious sanctions on the status of women. The changes in the focus of the studies demanded greater involvement of a variety of disciplines and thus inter-disciplinary and multi-disciplinary approaches have been tried. What was once primarily the monopoly of Indologists, anthropologists, and social historians has become more the concern of economists, sociologists, behavioural scientists, lawyers, doctors, demographers and political scientists.

During the last ten years, the issues which received great attention are women and work, women's labour force participation, women's participation in economic activity, women's unequal access to education, problem of employed women etc. Case studies of profiles of women workers in specific regions have emerged. Implication of modernization and industrialization on women, women's work, women's income and health, various aspects of female poverty—its incidence, pattern and impact, decision making in rural households, female headed households etc., have been attempted.

In recent years, gender Inequality has become the most important area. Violence in the home, dowry, dowry deaths, rape and sexual abuse, abuse of women in the media, sex role stereo typing in literature are the many issues which are being analysed.

Cash values for women's work in the household, integration of women in development, Women's involvement in public and community affairs are some interesting areas which are attracting the attention of the researchers and some interdisciplinary teams are working on these.

We can see, how studies on women were first very general, discipline oriented, descriptive and survery types, using essentially the technique of documentary/content analysis. The focus then shifted from macro to micro and from general to particular using more sophisticated tools and techniques such as questionnaires, in depth interviews, case studies and participant observation. Inter disciplinary and cross disciplinary approaches, integrating quantitative methods with qualitative interpretations are now being attempted. Action research methodologies are being used essentially for analysing and solving some specific problems related to women.

Some suggestions regarding the methodological aspects for research pertaining to women's studies are:

1. Methodologies should be evolved which would play a significant role in theory building; It is necessary to link the particular with the general and to place in-depth micro studies at regional levels in the broader prospectives and evolve locally relevant concepts and theories.
2. The existing theories should be reconceptualized and changed with the changing times.
3. Inter-regional comparisons using quantitative methods should be used to develop macro data base.
4. Cross country researches would play a significant role in expanding the scope of the theoretical research.
5. Women's studies should not be just another aspect of academic research but the content of the research should have some relevance to the condition of women studied. Participant improvement should be inbuilt in the methodology.

References

1. "Towards Equality", Report of the Committee on Status of Women in India, Government of India, 1975.
2. Conference Reports, The Latin American Seminar On Women's Studies Rio De Jeneiro, Brazil, Nov. 24-27, 1981.
3. Conference Reports, The National Conference On Women's Studies SNDT University, Bombay, 20-24, April, 1981.
4. Conference Reports, The National Conference On Women's Studies, Trivandrum.
5. Women's Studies International, November 2, July 1982.

DEVELOPMENT AND ADVANCEMENT OF WOMEN IN MANAGEMENT

1.00 The Setting

Although significant gains have been made in the last 15 years in increasing the number of women in entry level management positions, many women in junior positions still find that 'invisible ceilings' exist in their advancement into senior management positions. In the USA, while 15% of women currently work as managers, only 1% occupy senior positions.

Baroness Lackwood, the immediate past Chairman of Equal Opportunities Commission of U.K. , in her foreword to the book 'Women in Management' (1984) by Cary L. Cooper and Maretyn Davidson says 'Yet now, in the early 1980s, the fact is that women at the top are still noticeable by their scarcity: the 1982 "New Earnings Survey" shows that women were just below 1 in 40 of top earners which is very marginal improvemnent on the 1968 figures showing that women were just over 1 in 50 of the top earners, and in managerial positions as a whole, women are still a small minority with only approximately 9% of managers being women'. She asks, what has happened to all those women who set out on the right road during the last decade?

In our country, according to the report of the AIMA,

1. In the national recruitment scene, out of an over all 10% increase only 2% are women. They provide for only 12% of the total work force with continual dropouts, women executives are a miniscule proportion.

2. In the Government service, the proportion of women is only 6% in all civil services, 7.5% in the IAS and 10% in the foreign service. In the Indian Police Service, women's employment has increased from one in 1972 to 21% at present.

3. "According to the 'Profile of Women in Tamil Nadu' (1985), in judicial service, at the level of judges, sub judges and magistrates, for every 40 men, there is just one woman.

4. In the Legislative Assembly the proportion of women: men is 1:18
5. According to a report of the Association of Indian Universities, New Delhi, (1987),

Among the University teachers, there is one female teacher for every 10 male teachers.

In the research institutions, the ratio is 1 : 9

In colleges of general education, the ratio is 1 : 4

In colleges of professional education, the ratio 1 : 6

Among professors in the Universities, women constitute hardly 2%. There are about 10 women Vice-Chancellors out of total of 179 Vice-Chancellors of Universities and Deemed Universities.

(4 in Tamilnadu, 2 in Maharastra, 1 in Andhra Pradesh, 1 in Madhya Pradesh, 1 in Bihar, and 1 in Uttar Pradesh)

2.00 Barriers to Women's Advancement into Senior Positions

There have been quite a few research studies on this in USA, U.K. Australia and in India.

Bette Woody (1985) in her project 'Examples of Success' examined policy and program measures which have been provided most effective for advancing women into executive level decision making positions in the USA and she reports that an influence can be exerted by corporate settings on women's mobility to the top.

Studies on 'Why don't as many women as men go for promotion? by the South Australian Institute of Teachers (1980) have identified the following reasons:

1. Many women see promotion as 'beyond them' because of poor self image and low self esteem; females are conditioned to be dependant, non assertive and non leaders.

   Margaret Mead says 'In Western Society, men are unsexed by failure, women by success'.

2. There is a sense of guilt to deal with the implication, that to succeed, you must be causing harm to your real responsibilities—children, husband and home.
3. Women are not experienced in the 'Politics of the Job'; they do not tend to march forward for career advancement.

4. Men take their career seriously, as they are considered to be the bread winners; women's earning are seen as extra.
5. Broken services due to child bearing and child rearing affect promotion opportunities.
6. Women do not opt for transfer because of domestic responsibilities .
7. There are very few role models to offer support.
8. Male hierarchy tends to pass on promotion through the male line.
9. There is hidden discrimination against women.

A large scale study by Cooper and Davidson (1982) in U.K. reports that female managers are subjected to a greater number of pressures as compared to male executives. That the pressures stem, from stresses in the work, home, social and individual areas and there are more manifestations of psycho-somatic symptoms and poorer work performances by women compared to men managers.

They add that a majority of additional pressures at work experienced by female managers are stresses beyond their control and based largely on prejudice and discrimination from both organisational/corporate policy and other people at work.

Geeta Chaturvedi (1985) in her study, on women administrators of India, concludes that women lag behind that of men with similar initial performance and the barrier to women's advancement are the conflict between family responsibilities and career commitments, systematic gender inequality and the hidden processes.

Medha Dubashi Vinze (1987) studying the women entrepreneurs of India, reports that women lacked confidence to study their own ventures; social presure restricting freedom of movement, society's, lack of confidence in women and financial organisations not encouraging the women entrepreneurs are the reasons for women's unwillingness to come forward to take up entrepreneurship.

M.J. Lousis (1988) in her study on 'Women Executives of Tamil Nadu', interviewed bank executives, doctors, engineers, business women and educational administrators and their problems are identified associetal pressures, familial pressures and professional pressures. Guilt feeling of neglecting household responsibilities, tension and comflict with family members, fear of socieity, fear of transfer, lack of support services, lack of opportunities for training, lack of continuing educational facilities for professional growth and upgradation of skills have been identified as factors contributing of the pressures.

Majorie Lyles (1983) groups the barriers that stand in the way of effective development of women managers as arising from three primary areas, namely, socialisation process, lack of political awareness and tokenism.

Socialisation

Sex role stereotyping, male-female interaction pattern in the work place and the societal norms interact with each other and enhance each other. Women are supposed to stay at homeraise the children, women are better at nurturing, women are soft, loving, attending and intuitive are the accepted stereo-types and hence they are perceived as being afraid of achievement, poor at qualitative analysis and unable to make tough decisions. They are also perceived a being emotional, irrational and non-objective. Though these stereo-types are false, they subtly influence decision making about women in the work place.

Lack of Political Awareness

The political system or net work is already established in the organisation and without access to information about the implicit norms, power coalitions and acceptable srategies, accomplishment of the golas may not be possible. Women lose sight of the fact that it is not enough to be good at your job, but you must also be effective in terms of learning to operate within the organisation's informal power structure.

Tokenism

Only a few women make it to the senior positions and they are usually placed in the position of respresenting womankind and thus they become a token. Being a token creates a pressure on the individual woman-pressure to exce and pressure of isolation. Token women can also make male groups draw close together, making it uncomfortable for the women.

3.00 Helping Strategies

The questioin is how to move women along, out of tracks, out of dead-end positions, and into senior management. Search procedures should be changed, communication net works established and professional development programmes implemented.

(1) The number of women in administrative position can increase only when people in authority make affirmative action, an institutional imperative. The governing boards must make the advancement of women a publicly stated personal and institutional committment. Positive recruitment strategies, change in organisational procedures to remove the hurdles and obstacles which divert or block the progress, objective appraisal, a machinery for sharing information, establishing social contact which builds on net working, opportunities for developing interpersonal skills such as confidence, woking in groups, net working, trust, openness and assertiveness, training in women's issues such as women's rights, accuracy of stereo-types, statistics about women and their contribution to economy provision of role models, providing a mentor, training in new technology, retraining schemes, maternity and paternity leave, day-nursery facilities, flexible working arrangements such as flexi-time, flex-place etc. would be some of the measures the organisation can introduce for assisting women in their advancement into upper management positions.

(2) Women themselves must make a commitment to their own advancement. They must have the appropriate credentials, understand the organisational structures and political processes of the institution.

They should develop their own networks—organisation based, personal as well as professional.

To facilitate learning the rules of the game, they should have inner circle support by way of a mentor, man or woman.

Women also need to learn to cope with stress, combine and organise femily responsibilities with office work effectively, to relax as well as be efficient. A good manager has to win friends and influence people. It is not enough to do a good job but a woman has to outperform others, make her successes known, try and act as some one with management potential, convey such attributes as smartness, positive and confidential manner, achieve credibility as efficient, reliable, sensible and practical, develop resilience to criticism, and be wiling to take risks.

Despite difficulties, such as lack of support from the family, society and the government, and moments of self doubt, women must continue to strive to reach positions of influence and power, so that their capabities and intelligence are used to the full.

References

Ann Stead Bette - Women in Management, Prentice Hall, New Jersey, 1985.

Chaturvedi G. - Women Administrators of India, RBSA Publications Jaipur, 1985.

Cooper C. Land Davidson M. - Women in Management, William Heinemann Ltd., London,1984

Louis M.J. - Women Executives of Tamil Nadu, unpublished Project Report, NIEPA, Delhi.

Mike Smith (etal) ed - A development programme for women in Management, Gower, 1984.

Vinze Medha Dubashi - Women Entrepreneurs in India, Mittal Publishers, Delhi,1987.

WOMEN AS AGENTS OF TRANSFORMATION IN THE FIELD OF EDUCATION

This can be considered from two aspects:

(1) How can education make women become agents of transformation, and

(2) How can educated women become agents of transformation of the educational system itself.

What is desirable transformation? The ultimate end of education is to create better human beings who can make their world a better place to live in. Women's role in contemporary society is to transform society for the better.

Exceptionally gifted women in India have made individual contribution to education and society but the vast majority of women have been deprived of the opportunities to develop their potential to full capacity. Since women are considered as prime movers of the society, their education should assume greater relevance in the process of the development of the Society.

Literature and History are rich with names of many women who have been responsible for transformaation of society of their times in some way or other. In Tamil literature, Kannagi, an ordinary woman had the audacity to question the wisdom of the reigning king. Manimekalai, hundreds of years go, brought a silent revolution in the life of the prisoners.

In English literature Portia was acclaimed as the Daniel who came to give judgement; John of Arc led the whole French Army.

If we turn the pages of History, we come across Jija Bai who shaped Shivaji and through him the Maratha country; Rani of Jhansi who started the war of independnce, Kasthurba who stood shoulder to sholulder with Gandhiji in all his endeavours, Sarojini Devi who fianned the independence movement with her fiery poems, Sarada Devi, a beacon of light in spiritual field, Vijayalakshmi Pandit, Indira Gandhi and the living Saint Mother Theresa who is silently spreading the language of love and peace are all such examples.

What transformation do we need today in field of eduation?

The educational system in the present form has actually helped to perpetuate values and norms that thrive on the subordinate position of women. We should think in terms of how education can bring about speedy economic and social development and rid the society of its traditional weakness and social injustices; how education can change the lives of Indian women by developing their competence, capabilities and creativity.

How to revolutionalise the educational system so that it would stimulate social transformation is the question:

(1) Education can be utilised as an instrument to transform social values and practices that obstruct women's journey to equality. On the one hand it can contribute to structural changes and on the other it can generate new values that could create a new cultural ethos. So incorporation of problems and perspectives of gender discrimination as a legitimate area of concern in higher education would be a healthy development. The type of education that is imparted to women should enable them to participate successfully in the process of decision making.

(2) *Preparation for their dual role of home maker and wage earner:-* It is a well established fact that there are no basic differences in intelligence between the sexes and women can succeed at almost any job a man can do.

The failure to make effective use of women power reserves in the economic life of the nation, the failure to develop its women power fully through education and training and the failure in many instances to reward the female workers appropriately are some of the failures of our system.

An increasing number of women is working outside the home and the proportion of employed women may be expected to increase in the foreseeable future. They may be expected to enter few fields, including those stereotyped as men's occupation.

Employed women will also be home makers and hence they need to be prepared for a dual role.

(3) Education a system has been divorced from social reality, catering only for individual's upward mobility; it has been perpetuating existing social order with unemployment and unequal distribution of nation's resources.

There have to be cognitive changes, attitudinal changes and behavioural changes among the educated women. Education has to be an active generator of values not merely a passive adjuster to them.

Education should enable the students to rise in protest against injustice, oppression and neglect, marginalization and discrimination.

Holistic growth of the students is needed; so far only irrelevant knowledge has been forced into the heads of students killing creativity, originality and experimental minds of the students.

(4) The existing curriculum of higher education ignores the women's point of view.

History that is taught today ignores women's contribution; Economics ignores women's work at home and the farm and brands this work as non productive labour.

> Education fails to address itself to educating girls to promote equality; Sociology does not question the discriminatioin and oppression of women in society; Psychology ignores the strength of Women and Law reveals a bias against women; thus all these are distorted disciplines. Curriculum should dispel myths, prejudices, beliefs and practices which do not treat men and women as equals. This is necessary for raising women's self esteem which will help them to help themselves. Very little is known about the large majority of women who are invisible and whose contribution to development is considerable. This information is necessary for policy making. Women must be made visible in the curriculum.

The women of India should be trained to spearhead changes in their homes as well as in the communities. They must be made aware of their rights and wider responsibilities.

SECTION-II

4

WOMEN PROFESSIONALS AND EMPOWERMENT

Women Professionals—The Study

Women Physicians

Women Engineers

Women Lawyers

Women Managers

Women Professionals—Suggestions for Advancement

WOMEN PROFESSIONALS—THE STUDY

Education in India, for a long time was dissociated from the idea of nation building. It was viewed as a process for infusing piety during the ancient period. It was then seen as a cultural process, to transmit the accumulated wealth of knowledge, to impart classical values and to build the character of the individuals. It was essentially for a privileged few and hence was not really contributory to the development of the nation as we understand to-day. When the demand for women's education started in the 18th century it was more in the light of women's rights, for the access to knowledge and not as a national economic asset.

According to the statistics available regarding professional education of women in 1901-1902, the number of women students in training schools was 1412, medical schools was 166, technical and industrial schools was 468 and commercial schools 26. Of all the carrers then open to women, teaching was obviously the most popular. Next to teaching, medical career, such as nursing, midwifery and medicine were popular. The necessity of women doctors began to be felt very early as Indian women were naturally averse to consulting male doctors. The best achievement during the first quarter of this century was that there was large number of women teachers in general and trained teachers in particular. In 1921-22, the number of women in training schools rose to 4391 as against 1412 in 1901-02.

A great social and political awakening unequalled by that in any preceding period occurred among women in the two decades following the first world war and this led to a great improvement in their social position. In the social field, the age of marriage was now rising fast particularly among the upper classes of Hindus in urban areas.

In the national field, women had already obtained the right to vote in elections to local bodies and they could also be elected as representatives of local bodies. Another factor which helped the development of education among women was the new leadership that was now rising in their midst.

Gandhiji's contribution to the emancipation of women also was phenomenal. He was a staunch advocate of the equality of men and women and this had a great impact in all walks of life. The freedom struggle under Gandhiji's leadership attracted many women to enter politics and this also did considerable service to elevate the status of women. Women took part in the non-cooperation movement of 1921, the civil disobedience movement of 1931 and the Quit India Campaign of 1942; they fought shoulder to shoulder with men and won their emancipation as a tribute of gratitude. A specially important feature of their emancipation was the emergence of middle class women from the shelter of their homes.

Constitutional directives of non-discrimination on grounds of sex in employment and the specific directives to promote with special care, educational and economic interests of the weaker sections of the people had a direct bearing on the employment of middle class women. Greater opportunities to obtain higher education increased the employment opportunities in the organised sector and there was greater demand for women professionals, especially teachers, doctors and nurses; there was great pressure on middle class families in urban areas for enhancing the family income; these are all features of post independant India. The emphasis on women's equality that emerged during the freedom struggle had also influenced the attitude and aspirations of the educated middle class women.

The processes of modernization, industrialisation and urbanisation also had their impact on women's employment. One of the most important features of the developed and technologically advanced societies of the present age is the high rate of mobility and social change. In the developing countries also, societies were changing but gradually and slowly, because of the dead weight of traditionalism and social-cultural barriers. The processes of modernisation have accelerated social change and have been forcing Indian women into new social roles.

Modernisation refers to an inherent change in the mode of life. It involves not only changes in the material culture of a nation but also its beliefs, values, norms and way of life as a whole.

In traditional Indian Societies, women were economically and socially dependent on their fathers till marriage, on the husbands after marriage and on the sons later. They were mostly confined to household affairs and they were not allowed to participate in the political and economic affairs of the society. But with independence and attempts at modernisation, sex bias and discrimination have been done away with, and the concept of equality of the two sexes have been widely propagated and honoured.

The rapid industrialisation also created gereral employment opportunities from which women have benefitted. Though they are mostly employed at the lower levels, in unskilled occupations, it has helped them to become economically independent. There has been an increase in the number of home-based women workers. The process of urbanisatiion enabled girls to get exposed to education, information, health care, drudgery reduction and employment opportunities.

After independence, the possibility of employment under government provided a great stimulus for women's higher education. The demand for equality gradually broke the resistence of educational authorities and engineering, technical and vocational institutions which have been the monopoly of men till now, were opened out to women.

In short, industrial expansion, migration to urban areas, technology changes, western education and awareness of better standards of life etc. enabled women, especially middle class, urban, educated upper caste women to take up work outside in significant numbers and this economic activity outside home helped them to experiene financial and psychological independence to a certain extent. But it must be accepted that with a very few exceptions in the higher strata of society, majority of women took to working outside the home for economic reasons; men supported women's employment to augment the family's income. Rising prices, increasing cost of housing and education, aspiration for a higher standard of living increased the economic pressure on the middle class women.

2. Educational Achievements of Women since Independence—Selected Statistics

Since independence, there has been a steady increase in overall enrolment of girls in schools as well as improvement in gross enrolment ratio.

Enrolment percentage of girls in the age group 6-11 years which was 24.6 in 1950-51 increased to 66.4 in 1973-74. In the age group 11-14 years, the percentage of girls increased from 4.5 in 1950-51 to 22.2 in 1973-74. The following figures taken from the census reports on percentage of literate women give insight into the development of women's education.

Year	Percentage of Literate Women
1891	0.5%
1901	0.7%
1911	1.1%
1921	1.9%
1931	2.4%
1941	6.9%
1951	7.93%
1961	12.95%
1971	18.72%
1981	24.88%
1991	39.29%

Women's literacy is still way behind male literacy which has increased from 39.51% in 1971 to 64.13% in 1991.

In 1971 more than three fourths of the children who were not enrolled in school were girls. It has now decreased to 60% but it is still a very unsatisfactory position.

There has also been a rapid increase in higher educational opportunities and female enrolment in higher education has gone up by more than thirty points since 1951. The number of women in higher education in 1951 was 40000 and by 1988, it increased to 12 lakhs, an increase by 30 times. In the last four decades, the proportion of women to every hundred men at the university stage has increased from 14 in 1951 to 46 in 1988. In the colleges of general education, in 1950-51, there were only 14 girls for every 100 boy students, in 1960-61, it was 17 girls for every 100 boys and in 1965-66 it went upto 25 girls for every 100 boys. Of all students enrolled in higher education, 32.5% are girls today.

There has also been a change in the trends of the courses taken by women. More and more women have started taking up science, commerce and other professional courses.

According to figures available for 1991, inrolment of girls in science courses has increased to 33.3% and in commerce to 20.8%. In 1971, out of a total of 45000 science graduates, 81800, i.e. 18% only were women.

In professional courses at College level, there were only 5 girls for every 100 boys in 1950-51; in 1961,14 girls for every 100 boys were getting training in professional courses. One sector of higher professional education where women have come in large numbers is medicine. In 1971, 20% of the total number of medical students were women. The total number of girls enrolled in Engineering and Technology in 1971 was hardly 1051 students, i.e., less than 1% of the total enrolment. 8.5% of the law students, 4.6% of the agricultural college students and 5.2% of vaterinary college students were women. In 1988, 31% of the total enrolment in medical sciences were women and women practicing medicine were 26%. To-day, 35% of all physicians in India are women. Girls started to enter engineering institutions in significant numbers only after 1980. In 1988, 7% of the total entrants into engineering colleges were women and in law, it was 8.5%.

In ten years, i.e., by 1987, enrolment of girls increased by three times in engineering and one and a half times in medicine. The 1991 enrolment figures of women are 32.3% in medicine, 7.9% in Engineering, 8.2% in veterinary science, 7.2% in agriculture and 10% in law.

3. Occupational Distribution of Women

A significant trend in women's occupational pattern since independence is the increasing entry of women workers into non traditional services and professions. Non discriminatory opportunities for higher education, equality of opportunities in employment, changing social values, rapid industrial expansion, better economic development etc. gave opportunities for urban literate women to take up employment outside the home in considerable numbers.

The number of women in the various professional categories has been continuously increasing since 1960. Women administrators, executives, managerial workers also increased from 10000 in 1960 to 18000 in 1966. Women in clerical cadre in government registered a phenomenal increase from 37000 in 1960 to 79000 in 1968. Concentration of women in profession of teaching and nursing continued to increase and according to 1966 censes, 70% of the educated women were teachers, 7% were nurses, 11.8% were clerks, and only 1% were physicians. According to an I.L.O. study made in 1970 only 1.7% of the professional and technical workers were women of which, three-fourths were teachers.

Since 1970, there has been a change in the trend of the courses taken up by women. New job opportunities were opened up in industries, such as pharmaceutical, food processing and other chemical industries and women started going in for science; the classification of occupation of women according to 1971 census was that there were 60000 teachers, 2000 physicians,1700 lawyers, 700 engineers and 2500 were medical technicians in nursing and health care. In relation to men, the proportion of women in their selected occupation were as follows:

Physicians	7.1%
Teachers	30.3%
Lawyers	1.2%
Health Technicians	72.2%
Scientists	10.9%

The data supplied by the Ministry of Social Welfare for 1978 is that for every 100 males, were the number of women was

Supreme court judge	0
High court judge	2
I.A.S.	9
I.P.S.	0.09
Indian Education Service	5
Engineers	12
Doctors	25

Out of 23700 persons working as proprietors, directors and managers in business, in 1971, only 5300 were women. In 1991, women executives are still a miniscule proportion, less than 1%. In Government services, the proportion of women is only 6% in all civil services, 7.5% in I.A.S. and 10% in the foreign services. In the Indian Police Service, Women's employment has increased from 1% in 1971 to 21% in 1988. In the judicial service at the level of judges, sub judges and magistrates for every 40 men, there is just one woman.

Among the university teachers, there is one female teacher for every 10 male teachers; in the research institutions the ratio is 1:9, in colleges of professional education the ratio 1:6 and in college of general education, the ratio is 1:4. Among professors in the universities, women constitute about 2%; out of 179 vice chancellors of universities and institutions deemed as universities, there has not been more than 10 women at any one time. The proportion of seats won by women to the Lok Sabha in 1988 was 46 out of 537 seats. The Rajya Sabha had 28 women in a house of 245 seats. The pattern is similar at the State level also. In 1991 general election, women accounted for just 33 of the 503 members of parliament elected, which is a dismal 6.6%. Thus women's participation in politics has been quite poor.

If we take working women in general, 80% of the working women are in the primary sector as agricultural labourers and cultivators, 18% are factory workers and only 2% constitute professonals in higher salary brackets. Self employed women entrepreneurs, managers in business etc. are very few as women have little control on the productive resources. Thus very few women happen to be in a position to influence political thinking or decision making process.

In the Indian Police Service, employment has increased from 1% in 1972 to 21% to-day. Women have entered all the so called male dominated professions including military services, police forces, aviation and piloting and business management. All administrative positions are open to them on a competitive basis. The guarantee of the rights envisaged in the Constitution have enabled the women of modern India to enter all walks of life and make an imprint of her presence.

4. Condition of Women World Wide—Selected Statistics

In 1980, UNESCO issued a report which stated that "women make up half of the World's population, work two thirds of the total working hours, and yet receive only one tenths of the income and own only one hundredth of the world's property".

Later in 1993, U.N. reports indicated that in the whole of the 20th century, upto and including 1993, there are only seven women elected as Presidents and sixteen appointed Prime Ministers of the female gender, world wide. Among the legislative bodies, women on an average, occupy 10% of the seats. As to the cabinet level, the percentage is even lower, only 3.5%. Thus fewer than 10% of the seats in all parliaments world wide are fielded by women, 3.5% in ministerial postings and fewer than 5% in high level postings in international organisations, including the U.N. and European community.

Worldwide, 19.4% of all male and 33.6% of all women are illiterate.

Women earn on average, 30 to 40% less than men even in industrialised countries.

Women's incomes are considerably lower because they are employed in a limited range of badly paid jobs with a law productiveness rate. They work in jobs which do not get the recognition they deserve in national affairs.

Why is it that women, as tax payers and voters are not represented as they should be and often are not recognised by the Government? Obviously, these are problems with regard to concepts, cultures, systems and policies.

In spite of all the socio political economic changes, including the changes in attitude of men, despite the findings of psychological studies that women are not less intelligent or less capable, the number of educated women getting into employment is still comparatively very small, especially in top salaried occupations and decision making positions. What are the problems they face? What are the obstacles they have to encounter?

How empowered are the women professionals? Who choose to enter professional colleges? Why? Do the socio economic educational background of women influence their career choice? By whom are career decisions made? What factors influence the career decisions? Who are their role models? What is the career development like? Do women lag behind that of men with similar initial performance? If so, why? What are the barriers to women's true participation in the profession? Have women professionals made use of the opportunities provided to them to make a success of their career? How far do the family responsibilities clash with career commitments? What problems do the women professionals face at home? What problems do they face at work because they are women? Have women professionals made a significant contribution to the society especially in eradication of social ills which women face in our society? What are their attitudes towards social issues of women? Who are the successful women professionals? Is it possible to analyse the anatomy of success?

Four categories of women professionals, namely women physicians, women engineers, women lawyers and women at the managerial cadre were chosen and the research studies done on these categories were reviewed, analysed and synthesised to find out the answers for the queries raised above. The following chapters describe the findings.

WOMEN PHYSICIANS

1. Introduction

At the time of the advent of the British rule, the position of women in India was at its lowest ebb. Purdha system restricted the movement of women outside the home In the face of constant invasion it was difficult for the parents to protect their young daughters and this led to the undesirable practice of child marriage. The inhuman practice of Sati or burning alive of a widow on the pyre of her dead husband was in vogue. Female literacy was considered as a source of moral danger. The status of women was quite low; polygamy was prevalent among most communities. There was a general neglect of women's health. Child marriage led to child mothers and with illiterate untrained 'dais' attending deliveries, there was high incidence of maternal as well as child mortality. Indian women were naturally averse to consulting male doctors for any of their ailments and this was enforced by customs and religion. Child birth was considered virtually unclean and the young mother to be was usually confined to the darkest corner of the house. The necessity of women doctors was felt very acutely and it was the missionaries who provided the necessary services.

Dr. Clara Swain of Castile, New York, was the first medical missionary in the world. She was sent by the Methodist Church in 1869 to India and she began work by opening a small dispensary at Bareilly. The Nawab of Rampur who strongly advocated the service of women doctors gave her an estate of 40 acres to start the first hospital for women in India.

Perior to this, efforts were made to train Indian women in the Medical college of Madras but the proposal was turned down by the faculty. In 1875, for the first time, in the history of India, four women were admitted to the medical college at Madras. A great agitation was afoot to get women admitted into Calcutta Medical College but the Bengal public opinion was not ripe for such a move. The Bengal women moved to Madras to study medicine. Bombay admitted women in Grant Medical College in 1883. In 1885 Calcutta Medical College also opened up for women. Initially women attended classes sitting behind a curtain and the instruction of women in men's Medical colleges was not satisfactory. Demands for establishing separate medical colleges for women were made by many. The British Government, missionaries and the social reformers consciously attempted to encourage women to enter medical profession.

Braving public opposition, some pioneering women joined medical colleges. Mrs. Anandi Bai Joshi had the distinction of being the first Hindu woman to study medicine. She went to women's

Medical College at Philadelphia in 1883 and graduated in 1886. Annie Jagannathan and Mrs. Rukma Bai, in spite of public opposition to cross the seas, went to England and returned to take over the women's ward in Bombay and Surat.

The opening of the London School of Medicine and the Royal Free Hospital in 1877 provided the impetus for the english women doctors and nurses to appear in India.

Dr. Sara Seward, Dr. Mary Seelye, Dr. Nancie Monelle, Dr. Sereh Norris were the other American Missionery doctors who came from Women's Medical College of Pensylvania. Before the end of the Century, scores of women doctors—American, British and Canadian served in various parts of India. During the eighties, more and more Indian women studied abroad and came to work in hospitals in India. One of the most famous missionary doctors who did termendous service to Indian woman was Dr. Ida Scudder. She started the Mary Taber Schell Eye Hospital at Vellore, pioneered the idea of a mobile clinic to treat the patients in the country side. She campaigned tirelessly in America, raised sufficient money to start a medical school for women. The biggest project of her life was the starting of Christian Medical College at Vellore in 1918, the most prestigious medical centre in the country to-day, comparable to the most advanced institutions in the world . Her real contribution is not actually the college and the hospital but the fact that she inspired many Indian girls to take to medicine in the spirit of service. This medical college became coeducational in 1947 by admitting men.

Lady Dufferin fund was created in 1885 and a number of Dufferin hospitals were opened and women physicians were provided scholarships to study medicine.

The Christian Medical school for women in Punjab was opened in 1890 in Ludhiana and was affiliated to Punjab University in 1917. Lady Hardinge Medical College in Delhi was established in 1916. The graduates from these colleges staffed the hospitals opened through the Dufferin fund. Nurses, midwives and hospital assistants as well as medical practitioners at the licentiate level were trained in the beginning.

By 1927, there were 181 hospitals staffed by women in India, 93 of these were conducted by missionaries.

The early schools were of the licentiate grade. They were given the title Licenced Medical Practitioners (LMP). As the years passed, efforts were made to revise the standard and they became affiliated to universities. According to the report of the Association of Medical Women published in 1929, there were 100 women students in Lady Hardinge College in Delhi taking the 7 years course; 60 at the Grant Medical College at Bombay and about 20 in Calcutta Medical College.

In 1931, there were about 3000 women medical practitioners. Its number rose to about 4000 in 1941. The number of medical colleges in India has phenomenally increased since independence. In 1946 there were 15 medical Colleges with an annual enrolment of 1200 students. By 1963, there were 75 colleges with an admission capacity of over 10,000 students and by 1969, there were 89 colleges with 33000 students—25,000 men and 8000 women. The Association of Medical women in its report in 1954, stated that there were 61000 physicians in India, 4452 of which were women.

According to Man Power survey of 1967-68 there were about, 1,20,000 doctors, of which 12,000 were women. But according to the census report of 1971, the ratio of women physicians including surgeons was only 7.1 per hundred men 23,800 women to 336300 men. The number of qualified doctors is however about 25 per 100 men. Women doctors practicing medicine showed a decline from 9.1% per 100 males in 1961 to 7.1 per 100 men in 1971. This is most probably due to women doctors dropping out of the profession after their marriage.

Though there is a large work force of doctors, considering the population of the country, it falls short of the needs of the country. The ratio works out to one doctor per 5000 population where as the ratio considered desirable in advanced countries is 1:1000.

In 1971, there were some 95 medical colleges in India admitting about 12,000 students and 9000 qualified every year. Out of this, about 25% were girls. About 2000 to 2500 lady doctors are added every year. In 1988, women joining medical schools was 31% and women practicing medicine was 26%. To-day 35% of all physicians in India are women. It is interesting to compare these figures with those of other countries.

In U.S.A. in 1960s only 6% of those entering medicine was girls. In 1970s it was somewhere between 7 and 10%, in 1980s it was between 10 and 16% and in 1985 it increased to 14.6%. The projected figure for 1990 was 33%.

In numbers, in 1951 only 400 women entered all of the nations medical schools. In 1970 there were only 22011 women physicians and in 1985, it tripled with 74772 women physicians. In 1979, 50604 women in 11% of the physician population were women. Among the statistics of the1970s, of all the free world countries, the United States was near bottom in the number of women physicians. The USSR had the highest percentage, with 70 to 80% of women physicians.

In Eastern Europe since world War II, 30% of the medical students have been women. In U.K. it is 25%, in Israel, 22.5% and in Philippines and Thailand, between 20 and 24%.

There was remarkable progress in women's medical education in U.S.A. after the seventies because of enactment of anti discrimination legislation in 1972, adoption of resolution on equal opportunity by the American Colleges in 1970 and the collective consciousness raised by the Feminist Movement. Since 1978, there has been no gender barriers to women entering medical schools.

The dignity of the medical profession has been established from early years in India. It has been accepted as a respective profession for women for a considerable period and the general tendency has been for women to specialize in the practice of gynaecology and obstetrics. Another fact worth observing is that women doctors served mostly in urban areas. 1971 figures indicate that 20-40% of the total number of doctors, practised in large urban centres such as Delhi, Bombay and Madras. Rural areas continued to suffer from a shortage of women doctors.

There have been numerous studies by research scholars on women physicians in India and abroad. A review and synthesis of the Indian studies by the following scholars —Abidi (1933), Annapurni (1986), Balfour and Young (1929), Blumburg and Dwaraki (1982) Chakraburthi (1978), Chapman (1984), Chaturvedi (1985), Gokilavani (1987), Gore (1982), Jaggi (1979), Kalarani (194), Kapur (1975), Krishnakumari (1987), Labra (1984), Lovejoy (1957), Muthuchidambaram (1990) Oommen (1979), Ramu (1977), Venkataratnam (1979) and Wasi (1972) and comparing these with the review and synthesis of the consensus of findings of national surveys, analog studies and behavioural studies on women physicians in the U.S.A during the seventies and the eighties by Cartwright and Mandelbaum (1970), Ducker (1978),

Davidson (1979), Elston (1977), Epstein (1981), Fidell (1980), Heins (1978), Horner (1972), Kanter (1976), Kaufman (1978), Kosa (1970), Lorber (1988), Meguire (1966), Martin Parker and Arnold (1987), Olson and Miller (1989), Pilpawin (1976), Pugh and Waterman (1983), Rosen-that (1979), Weismen (198), Wunderman (1980), and others give us the following picture:

2. Socio Economic, Educational Background

In India, during the forties, due to the influence of Christian missionaries, more Christian women entered medical schools; during that time the Hindus were quite conservative and were against girls taking up employment outside home. The Muslim women were strictly adhering to Purdha system and seclusion. During the fifties and sixties more Hindu women from forward caste and higher income groups, with consistent high academic record entered medicine and during the seventies, a few Muslim girls as well as Hindu girls from backward classes also joined medical education.

Most of the girls entering medical school were from high income groups in urban areas. Hardly 15% were from middle income and rural areas even in 1980. Studies have reported that there is a high correlation between education of parents and the educational attainment of their wards. Girls entering medicine had educated fathers from white collar occupations and about 40% of them were doctors. Only after the seventies, girls belonging to business families and agricultural families joined medicine. The minimum qualification of the mothers of about 80% of the girls entering medical school was matriculation.

During the seventies it is found that about 17% of the mothers were working women. The studies find that parents play a dominant role in setting the educational goals for their children. The father has stronger role to play in the matter as he has to decide whether money should be invested in the daughter's professional education or in marriage. The father is the strong role model. The educated parents who believed in women having a career sent their daughters for medicine. Ginsberg study in the U.S.A. find that 75% of women opting for medicine had working mothers.

Career Choice

In the forties and early fifties 50% of the girls entered medicine with service motive, about 41% for economic independence and about 8% for prestige reasons. During the sixties and seventies prestige and family traditions are quoted as reasons influencing the girls for choosing medical career and hardly 5-10% give service as a motive. The recent trend seems to be that the appeal of the profession and employment opportunities available influence the career choice. The career choice is mostly self choice and not much influenced by the parents.

Career Development

The traditional Indian values expect women to be subordinate, altuistic and self sacrificing. But the qualities needed in work life are competition, confidence and assurance. In Indian families, boys are encouraged and reinforced to develop masculine characteristics-aggression, dominance, independance, sense of adventure and achievement oriented where as girls are encouraged to acquire feminine characteristics such as being submissive, nurturing, dependant and less achievement oriented. It is also true that career or no career, gilrs are brought up with marriage as the goal. There is near cent percent marriage among women physicians in India.

The studies report that women did not have a strainght arrow path as men physicians had and they did not sustain their early accomplishement. By mid career, they lag behind men with similar intial performance. The reasons are found to be that the priority given to family demands were barriers to career development (Kalarani (1976), Lebra (1984) and Sinha (1989).

They had to accommodate to husband's careers and had to opt for positions compatible with their family roles. (Kapur 1984 and Sinha 1987).

Many Indian women refused transfers, promotions etc. as they did not want to move out and get separated from their families (Ramu 1977).

As the families do not permit women to live alone, spatial mobility gets reduced (Blumberg and Dwarki, (1982).

Her personal safety and security is in danger (Lebra 1984) and her chastity is questioned (Chathurvedi 1985, Srivatsav 1986).

Living alone is a social stigma and the husband's career is given priority (Lebra 1984, Chaturvedi 1985)

Due to women's preoccupation with marriage, family and child care responsibilities, career development is affected and this results in role strain and role conflict and sometimes they sacrifice career for family (Lober 1984).

Inspite of all these barriers, the researchers also report that married women doctors did batter than unmarried ones especially in establishing dispensaries, hospitals and private practice due to the support they received from their husbands and families. The specialization they chose were either in terms of women and children's diseases such as gynaecology, obstetrics, pediatrics or non-clinical specialities such as physiology, Anatomy or Pathology so that there would be fixed hours of duty, less tension and more compatibility to adjust to the family roles.

Those women physicians who married physicians expressed husband's positive attitude and support in having joint practice.

American studies confirm most of the findings of the Indian studies regarding career dvelopment. It is also found that there is more rigid gender typing of specialities in the USA, the typical women's speciality being pediatrics and the typical men's speciality being surgery (Elston 1980, Rosenthal 1979).

In the U.S. among practicing women physicians, in 1985, 68% worked in primary care fields: internal medicine, family and general practice, obstetrics and gynaecology, pediatrics or psychiatry. In contrast, only 44% of male physician practiced in these specialities (Martin, Parker and Arnold 1987).

As domestic help is very expensive, American women have more career interruptions; despite good performance and high grades in medical schools and internships at prestigious teaching hospitals, women physicians did not sustain their early accomplishments. By mid-career, their professsional attainment lagged behind men with similar initial performance. Heins (1976) reports that women physicians suffered from role over load, role conflict and felt that they had too many demands on their time and energy and hence very little time for themselves. Data from 1986 shows that only 52% of the women physicians were self employed in contrast to 77% men physicians. Women physicians averaged 73000 dollars annual net income compared to 118000 dollars by men.

5. Career Performance

Most of the studies from most of the countries on women professionals, in general, report that the aspiration level of women is not very high and that is the reason why most women end up at middle level leadership and hardly 1% rise to the top. Women are quite satisfied with their achievements even if they do not rise to the top.They have anxiety and fear of success and hence try to avoid success. They are not too much concerned about salary or promotion and are more interested with the atmosphere of the work place, and personal relationships. If self employed, women work less number of hours than men.

The medical work ratio, i.e., full time equated months in medical work since medical school graduation is calculated as 0.993 for men and for women it is 0.880. Women work less number of hours, about 70% of men's time and the median personal income is in the proportion of 40:60. Women physicians with children do show fewer hours worked and more career interruptions than male physicians but the over all or life time productivity is not that much lower. But professional productivity is not always the most significant factor influencing professional status.

Sinha, Kapur and Horner attribute women physician's lack of representation at the top levels of medical institutions to their modest ambition.

Studies which tested for success avoidance in women found many situations in which women were ambitious, especially in advancement in their own fields. Research on women in male dominated fields found that women could be equally competitive with men, given the right work environment. (Kanter, Epestein, Muthuchidambaram, Oomen, Dubey).

In India, women physicians who enter service either with Government or quasi government institutions work full time and as there is a salary scale, earn the same as men. But in private practice, they earn less due to their speciality, hours worked and the number of patients seen. In specialities like general surgery, cardiology, neuro surgery etc. which are male dominated, men earn much more. 85% of the Indian women, prefer to consult women physicians but men generally do not like to go to women physicians unless there is an emergency.

In the U.S.A., it is found that 58% men and 49% women prefer to consult male physicians and 40% have no preference for men or women physicians. One of the studies on preference reported that the respondents felt that women were more sensitive, more caring, more sympathetic, better in communication, they had better rapport and they were more respectful of patients' concerns whereas men were more assertive, curt and ignored patients' questions.

Career development of male physicians follows a progressive direct line with many factors contributing to professional attainment. The factors indentified are achievement motivation, medical school performance, faculty and peer recognition in medical school, internship location and family responsibilities. For women physicians, in spite of all academic parameters such as academic performance, award of honours and prestigious residencies being equal, because of family responsibilities, their scholarly productivity is less than men. Women physicians publish fewer papers than men; they are less mobile which is necessary for succeeding in academia. Women do not have mentors to encourage them. More men than women belong to professional organisations and they are more active in attending meetings.

Though there has been an increase in the number of women employed full time in medical school faculties, in promotion to assistant professors and a substantial increase of women in academic administration, still, not many women head medical colleges worldwide, including Soviet Russia where 75% of the physicians are women.

6. Professional Role Performance

Stereotypical physicians are supposed to have characteristics such as rationality, objectivity, technical authoritativeness and aggressiveness in face of emergencies. Women physician are supposed to embody characterisitcs such as compassion, personal involvement, patience and maternal authoritativeness. Whether women are a small or large percentage of physicians, the gender concentration in the different specialities is remarkably consistent from country to country with pediatrics, the typical women's speciality and surgery the typical men's. In Asia, Latin America and the Middle East, more women specialize in gynaecology and obstertics because of the modesty of female patients in these countries.

Due to sex typing and sex role expectations of the society on one hand and rights and duties expected from the professionals occupying a certain place in the heirarchy of the organisation, there is conflict between the occupational role expectation and feminine role expectation.

As Women's role is associated with home making, bearing and rearing of children and hence with attributes such as warmth, patience, empathy, grace, endurance etc. they are tracked into lower prestige work and not considered leadership material (Lober, Osaka, Venkatarathnam, Martin and Osmond etc.)

If a woman is successful in her occupation she is less successful as a woman (Muthuchidambaram, 1990, Brown and Klein, 1982) as there is incongruence between occupational role expectations and feminine role expectations. Sex role, sex role expectations and sex segregation do affect the professional performance of women physicians.

7. Barriers at Work

Almost all the American studies and some of the studies by Indian scholars indicate that there is overt and subtle gender discrimination. The findings on the hidden processes of gender discrimination of women physicians in the U.S. are probably generalizable to the experience of women physicians in other countries as well and many of these processes have been found in other professions also.

An adequate explanation of the under representation of women physicians at the top levels of the medical profession, the studies report, is not only because of their modest ambition, low prestige specialities, their relegation to family responsibilities but much more due to the 'sorting and sifting; process of sponsorship and patronage, the help and hindrance of colleagues, mentors and husbands. These factors are better able to explain after women physicians' success or lack of it.

The heart of the process in medical profession is sponsorship and patronage. Some of the male gate keepers do not yet believe that women have the capability to work as their men colleagues. The tendency is to offer opportunities for advancement to those similar to their own background. Women also seem to be unfamiliar with the game of self presentation; they are not able to negotiate themselves into important positions in the organisations and thus their worth gets ignored by their male colleagues and men in the larger professional net work. Thus women have to be better than men to attain the same status. (Pugh and Watermen 1983, Piliavin 1976, Olson and Miller 1989).

In recommendation of position, promotion, officership in professional associations etc. competence is often evaluated only in professional shop talk. As most of the women are soft spoken and reticent they are likely to be over looked. In the male dominated work world, self advancement in women is seen as aggressive and they are socially devalued as women. Successful careers in medicine are built on combination of sponsorship, visibility and reciprocal favours. The career trajectories of the physicians interviewed by Lorber (1984) show that professional development is as dependent on the action of colleagues and superiors as on the person concerned. (Annapurani (1986, Kalaranai (1987) report that Indian women follow a policy of avoiding unpleasant situations to avoid discrimination and harassment and hence do not go up the ladder in careers. Sex seggregation leads to inter action with colleagues of the same sex and thus women physicians become more dependent on their physician husbands for pursuing their careers.

8. Constraints at Home

Indian society is a tradition bound, male dominanted society and cherish values such as virginity, chastity, fidelity etc. Marriage is very important in the lives of Indian women and social attitude is against women remaining single. Parents consider arranging the marriage of their daughters—even when they are mature adult professionals—as their chief responsibility and this is made more complex when caste, community factors have to be considered. To-day women professionals are in great demand due to their potential for earning as well the prestige of the profession. Most of the women physicians marry men from the same profession or atleast with equal professional status (Annapurani, Kapur).

Women physicians consider family as their prime responsibility and managing of homes is done with the help from family members or hired help. Strong supportive family network is a positive factor in Indian setting enabling women professionals to combine work and career.

The question of husbands sharing domestic responsibilities or child care responsibilities does not arise as both physician husbands and wives consider men helping in these responsibilities as demeaning, report Kalarani (1876) and Sinha (1987). They also state that women professionals do feel guilty of neglecting their children and they regret that they do not have enough time to spend with their children.

But the women physicians in Government/quasi government service are entitled to 3 months maternity leave, medical leave and leave without pay etc. hence they are able to combine their career with domestic and child care responsibilities without career interruptions.

American studies also report that marriage brings with it problems of not having enough time for spouse, role over load and critical issues of the dual career family. The dual burden has affected women physicians for more than a century and continues to shape their career choices. This is reflected in the social world of men and women.

In the U.S, only two thirds of women physician were married in contrast to national average of 90% of female non-physicians. Only 60-70% of the married women Physicians had children in contrast to 90% of the male Physicians having children. Women Physicans had fewer children and they were older when they had their children (Martin, Parker and Arnold, 1987).

A 1982 study reported that 75% of the women physicians surveyed stated that they were personally responsible for most house work in their homes. Another 1983 study found that 50% of male physicians agreed with the statement that 'women physicians who spend long hours at work, neglected their responsibilities to home and family'. Between 30 to 60% of women physicians felt that family-career conflicts were important influences on their lives. Another study found that women explicitly sought regular and shorter working hours because of concerns regarding family life.

A plausible interpretation of all these data is that women choose lower prestige specialization, shorter working hours etc. as they are more amenable to integrating their personal and professional lives.

9. Attitudes of Women Physicians

American studies found that women physicians were generallv

more liberal and egalitarian than men physicians. Older women were more liberal than older men and younger men were closer in attitudes to young women. 'Egalitarian' included attitudes about equality in occupations, domestic responsibilities, domestic decision making and appropriate gender role behaviour. Liberalism included attitudes towards reducing costs for patients, positive attitude towards welfare policies such as maternity leave, part time internship etc., racial tolerance, liberal sex role orientation, efforts to overcome race and sex discrimination, banning of nuclear weapons, abortion laws, pre marital sex etc.

Regarding the attitudes of Indian women physicians towards social issues, Indian studies report that women physician are found to be positive in their attitude towards women's movement, concept of equality of both sexes, prohibition of dowry, property rights for women, intercaste marriage, widow remarriage, legalisation of abortion and liberal sex role orientation thus confirming that they are rational in their thinking.

10. Conclusion

There has been a striking demographic shift in the profession of medicine. 35% of all physicians in India are women. Women now practice in virtually every medical speciality though the traditional differences in the choice of speciality still continue. The number of women entering medical profession is increasing but their accession to senior faculty positions has not kept pace. They lack role models and mentors. Women physicians are struggling to combine a medical career with raising a family. Subtle forms of sex discrimination still remain active. Research on women in male dominated fields found the women could be equally competitive with men, given the right environment. Persistent and pervasive gender discrimination rooted in the status of women in male dominated society still keeps women in the lower or middle level careers in spite of their competence and capability.

Better networking, patronage and sponsorship and higher visibility are needed for women to be successful in their career. Whatever the obstacles, women are found to perform as well as men; the percentage of women entering surgery and surgical specialities has increased; the number of women in medical school faculties has increased; there has been substantial increase in the number of women in academic administration. Recent pressures against sex discrimination has brought about positive changes. Support structures such as reliable child care services, hostels for working women, subsidised health care, creches, day care centres, senior citizens hostels, social security measures etc. are recommended to help the women physicians in executing their occupation roles better.

References

Abidi-N.F., Women physicians, Delhi: Manak publications Pvt. Ltd., 1993.

Annapoorni., A study of professional socialization of women medical and nursing students in medical colleges, unpublished Ph.D. dissertation, Madurai Kamaraj University, Madurai, 1986.

Balfour. M.I. and Young. R., The work of medical women in India, London; Oxford University Press, 1929.

Blumburg.R.and Dwarki. L., India's educated women, New Delhi; Hindustan Publishing Corporation, 1980.

Cartwright, L. and Mandelbaum., Conscious factors entering into the decision of women to study medicine, University of California, 1970

Chakrabarthi Krishna., The conflicting Worlds of Working mothers, Calcutta: Progressive Publications, 1978

Chapman. E.F., Notable Indian Women of the Nineteenth Century, New Delhi: Inter India Publications, 1984.

Chaturvedi Geetha., Women Administrators in India; A study of the Socio Economic background, Jaipur : RBSA publication, 1985.

Davidson.L.A.,Sex roles, Affect and the women physicians, Ph.D. dissertation New York University, 1979.

Dacker, D.G., Believed Suitability of Medical Specialities for women physicians, Journal of the American Medical Women's Association, 33 : 25-32,1978

Elston Mary Ann., Women in the medical profession: What problem? in Stacey etal(Ed) Health and the division of labour, London: Croom Helm

Epstein.C.F., Woman's place: Options and limits in professional Careers, Berckly, Cal: University of Califonia Press, 1970

Gokilavani. S., Reference group of doctors in an organised set up: A comparative study of two hospitals in Madurai city unpublished doctoral dissertation, Madurai Kamaraj University, 1987

Gore.M.S., Education and Modernisation in India, Jaipur, Rawat Publications, 1982

Grenel.B., Correlation of speciality choice of female medical students—Ph.D. dissertation, Columbia University, 1979.

Heins Merilyn., Current Status of Women physicians, International Journal of Women's Studies 1 : 297 - 305, 1978

Horner.M.S., Toward an understanding of achievement related conflict in women, Journal of social issues, 28 : 157-176, 1972

Jagge. O.P., Western medicine in India: Medical Research - History of Science, Technology and Medicine in India, New Delhi, Atmaram and Sons, 1979.

Kalarani., Role conflict in Working Women, New Delhi, Chitra Publications, 1976

Kanter. R.M., Men and Women of the Corporation, New York: Books Inc.,1977

Kapur Promila., The changing status of working women in India, Delhi, Vikas Publishing House, 1975

Kapur Promila., Marriage and working women in India, Delhi, Vikas Publishing House, 1978

Krishna Kumar.N.S., Status of Single Women in India, New Delhi Uppal Publishing House, 1987

Kosa. J., Enterpreneurship and Charisma in the medical profession, Social Science and medicine 4: 25-40, 1970

Labra Joyce., Women in medicine in Women and Work in India-Continuity and change, New Delhi, Pramila & Co., 1984

Lorber Judith., Women physicians; Career Status and Power, London, Tavistock Publications, 1984

Love Joy.,E.P., Women doctors of the world, New York, Macmillion 1957

Mcguire., A review of psycho social studies on medical students, 1966

Muthuchidambaram, professional women: a comparative study of women doctors and engineers, unpublished doctoral dissertation, Mother Teresa Women's University, 1990

National Conference of Women doctors in India., proceedings, New Delhi, 1975

Oommen. T.K., Doctors and nurses, a study in occupational structure, Delhi, Macmillion 1979

Piradova. M.D., USSR - Women Health Workers, Women and Health 1 : 24-29, 1976

Ramu. G.N., Family and Caste in Urban India: A case study, Delhi, Vikas Publications 1977

Rosenthal. M.M., perspectives on Women Physicians in the U.S.A., Internatiional journal of Women's studies 2 : 528-40, 1979

Sinha Pushpa., Role conflict among working women, New Delhi, Ammol Publications, 1987

Venkatarathnam. R., Medical Sociology in an Indian Setting, Madras, Macmillan, 1979

Wasi, M., Professional Women in India; Dangerous Corners, IIPO., Vol.18, No. 1 : 17-20, Oct. 1972

Weisman (etal)., Male and Female physician Career patterns speciality choices and graduate training journal of medical education 55 : 8, 13-25, 1980

Wunderman.L.E., Female physician in the 1970s, their changing role in medicine, in porfile of medical practice, Chicago, AMA center of Health Services Research, 1980.

WOMEN ENGINEERS

Indian Setting

Engineering Education in India was started in late 18th century. An engineering school was started in Madras in 1794 and it was upgraded into a college in 1857. Thompson Engineering College was started in 1847 at Roorkee, Calcutta Engineering College in 1856 and Indian Institute of Science at Bangalore in 1911. At the time of our independence, there were 38 Engineering Colleges with 2940 students and by 1957, the number of engineering colleges more than doubled, with 87 engineering colleges and 11510 students, as priority was given to technical education after independence.

The maximum increase in enrolment in engineering colleges has witnessed in the first decade 1950-60 in independent India. Growth of engineering colleges and enrolment of students is given below:

Year	*Engineering College*	*Enrolment*
1950	47	3800
1960	113	16000
1970	139	18200
1980	157	28500
1990	303	66500

The growth of enrolment in the last decade 1980-90 can be attributed to the emergence of self financing institutions which sprang up in the eighties. All India Institutes of Technology were established at Karagpur in 1951, at Bombay 1958, at Madras in 1959, Kanpur in 1960 and at Delhi in 1961. Besides these, Règional Engineering colleges also were established for accommodating more specializations. Women started entering engineering colleges only after 1948. Increasing employment opportunities, and growing prestige of the profession attracted women into engineering. By 1950-51 for 12094 men in the engineering faculty there were 19 women and by 1960-61, the number of men in engineering was 43389 and women was 403. In 1970-71, out of a total number of 90944 students, only 910 were women.

In percentage of total enrolment, enrolment of women in engineering and Technology was hardly 3.8% in 1980-81 and in 1988-89,it had increased to 6.2%. According to 1991 census, the enrolment of women in engineering colleges is only 7.9%

Other Countries

Comparing these figures with those of other countries, we find in technically advanced United States of America women comprised fewer than 1% in 1960 (Robin 1960).

In the mid seventies women entered engineering in significant numbers and by 1979, 9% of the Bachelor's degree recipients were women (Sheridan 1980) and by 1985, the number of women has increased to 14%. There were more women in medicine and law than in Engineering.

Women in England held high positions in science and technology even in 1964 and they had received recognition for their scientific achievements. The number of women in engineering and technology in the USSR is about 30% of the total number of Engineers; in Norway it is 9.8%, in Sweden 9.4%, in Federal Republic of Germany 4% and in the Middle East 9.5%.

In June 1964, the first international conference of women Engineers and Scientists was held in New York under the auspices of the American Society of women engineers. Out of 100 applicants, from 15 countries, there were 23 from U.K., from India and 8 from Japan. The Indian applicants held advance degrees, mostly from prestigious institutions in U.K. and U.S.A. Some of them had published papers and written chapters in technical books. These women came for the conference mostly to find out how women in Science and Engineering were recognised in the other countries, especially the host country, USA, the land of the Free. They were surprised to find that women in Science and Engineering had not made much advancement.

Who enters engineering colleges? What are the perceptions of women about engineering as a field? What are the experiences of women in the profession of Engineering in terms of their career development, career performance, barriers to career goals, career and family, combination, sex role expectation, role conflicts etc.? What is the attitude of these women engineers towards liberalism, egalitarianism and other buring social issues?

Studies Reviewed

A review of the studies done on women professionals in general and women Engineers in particular by the following scholars in India and abroad and a synthesis of the findings give us the picture described in the following pages.

The studies reviewed were by sister Benedicta Pinto (1993), Chakrabarthy (1978). Dass Dayal (1984), Data Sarita (1984), George Mary (1975), Indira (1989), Jaiswal Joshi (1956), Kalbagh (1992), Kalarani (1976), Silverstone and Pernel (1967), Sinha (1987), Srivatsav (1978), and studies on American women Engineers by Bernard (1970), Davis (1978), Haber (1981), Harrison (1981), Harrison Gay and Lutfer (1981), Hollander (1977) and Shafer (1981), Holmstrong (1975), Horst (1981), Kanter (1977), Lemkau (1979), Loring (1980), Medine (1981), Michael (1988) and Reese (1975), Ott (1976), Roby (1972), Robin (1961) Rossi (1965), Sheridan (1980), Spencer and David (1987), Tangri (1972), Wolman and Frank (1975), Yonalem Alice (1979).

There is only a small number of women in the profession of engineering due to three reasons says Jessie Barnard.

1. The attitude that engineering is an all male profession and therefore girls are counselled away from it.

2. Unwillingness of employers to hire women as they fear that they would lose them in marriage.

3. Several obstacles arising from sex difference in engineering work.

Studies done in India state that engineering education is generally a long and expensive course. Parents in India naturally prefer to spend their scarce resources to support their sons in engineering college. Many parents think that money spent on engineering education of the daughter brings no return to the family as she has to be married off. As a result, women students form a tiny percentage of the total strength in engineering colleges.

Other prejudices are that women do not have the stamina to prosecute engineering studies, that they do not have the adequate aeuman or talents for Mathematics which is the basis for engineering studies.

Socio Economic Background

Indian studies report that in the early stages women from upper middle class families and with consistent high academic record joined engineering colleges. They belonged to high income groups and had educated parents. Usually the father was the role model. During the fifties and sixties, mostly Christian girls and Hindu girls from the forward caste took advantage of engineering studies. During the seventies and eighties, Hindu girls from backward communities, as well as Muslim girls started entering engineering institutions. But even in the eighties, 83% of the girls entering engineering college were from urban areas and only 17% came from rural areas (Muthuchidambaram (1990). Majorily of the fathers were graduates and post graduates and 3% of them were engineers themselves. During the eighties, about 28% of the mothers of the engineering college girl students were working women; 22% of the mothers were graduates, 75% were matriculates and hardly 3% were uneducated mothers. This confirms the findings of the earlier studies on women professionals by Blumberg and Dwaraki Prasad, Krishnakumari, Chaturvedi, Pendey, Gore etc, that there was high correlation between education of parents and the level of educational attainment of their daughters. Parents played a dominant role in setting the educational goals for their children. The girls, when they finished school, were hardly 15-16 years, quite immature, they did not have adequate career information or vocational guidance, had limited worldly exposure, had no role models and held the value of obeying the parents and let them choose their careers.

Career Choice

Parental encouragement and marks obtained in the qualifying examination decided their entry into engineering courses.

Career choices and career decisions are influenced by the decisions about marriage, parenthood, female-male responsibilities in home making, social norms and expected sex roles. Women are not free to explore their interest and make choice with a conscious perspective. In most of the Indian families, even to-day, girls are not taken seriously as careerists and it is considered to be of secondary importance. Marriage is still, the principal determinent of women's social position. Sex role stereotyping influence women's lives from birth and it is a powerful influence in schools. This results in restrictions upon the freedom of occupational choice and career development of girls.

Currently the factors which influence girls to take to Engineering and Technology are the social status and prestige which goes with the profession and economic independence it would bring to them. This finding of Muthuchidambaram (1990) is supported by the findings of Horst (1981) who listed the factors of career choice in order of importance. The chance to earn a good deal of money, attaining social status and prestige, to look forward to a stable secure future and to use one's special abilities were cited as important reasons for choosing engineering studies.

Another common finding is that the role model of women who choose engineering was mostly the father and in the USA most of the women Engineers during the seventies had fathers who were engineers themselves according to Ott (1976) Horst (1981).

In India as well as USA and UK, the government are following an aggressive policy to attract more women into non-traditional jobs in engineering sciences. This is also one of the main reasons which encourage women to choose engineering.

Career Development

Women's career development depends on a number of factors. Due to women's preoccupation with marriage, family and child care responsibilities, there is role strain which leads to role conflict and career is affected. Usually career development is assessed in terms of promotion to higher cadres, improvement in knowledge and specialisation in the profession.

In the case of women engineers it is found that career options are restricted by the employment agency itself. There is reluctance on the part of private industries to employ women in their undertakings. Hence most of the women engineering graduates choose to join the goverment or quasi-government organisations or trust organisations. Women prefer government organisations as there is security of service, uniform service conditions, pay, position, increment, promotion etc. framed by rules and regulations; the only snag is that it is a transferable service. Many Indian women engineers, after marriage used to drop out of service in the seventies; some studies have also reported that they refuse promotions if they are transferred as they do not like to relocate. Unmarried women have more geographical mobility to avail better opportunities but they do not like to live alone on their own, as their personal safety and security is in danger (Blumberg and Dwaraki (1980), Lebra (1980).

Due to sex typing of the profession, 58% of the women used to choose Civil Engineering and they preferred desk work such as designing and drafting as it was considered that women were not tough enough to manage men workers in construction work. Less than 5% of the women engineers are found working outdoors, supervising construction work. Lober reports that there was more sex stereotyping among engineers than in any other professionals. Status wise, designing is considered less prestigious than teaching which is lower than execution of projects. Thus even highly qualified women end up in low prestige jobs.

The trend to-day is more women are choosing Electronics and Computer Engineering as they are mostly indoor jobs and also because job opportunities are better.

In the United States also, it is found that women entered Chemical Engineering more than Industrial Engineering and Electrical and Electronics more than Mechanical Engineering. Women work more in teaching and in research than in construction work or project work. (Horst 1981) reports that there is both access discrimination as well as treatment discrimination of women engineers. There is more difficulty for women than men in getting hired for a job. And once they get hired, they encounter less favourable conditions in the job in several settings including teaching jobs. Horst also reports that there is widely shared perception that sex discrimination is more in engineering than in other fields.

When women started engineering in the seventies, they confronted being the only ones in class rooms and laboratories; they were being singled out as tokens and being made to fit into sex role stereo types report Kanter(1971), Tavris (1977), Davis (1978), Wolman and Frank (1975). The positive consequences of tokenism are optimistic perception of the job market and some token women have managed to become successful 'Queen Bees'. Research on women entering non- traditional occupation such as Engineering suggests that these 'role innovators' are distincitve in a number of ways. According to Harrison (1981), they were high in self esteem; Mednic(1981) says that they contribute their success to internal causes; Lemkau (1978) says that they are independent, assertive and confident; and Ott (1976) finds them academically better qualified than their male peers. All these reports suggest that women engineers were deviant in a positive sense. A large number of American women engineers work part time so as to combine their domestic and family responsibilities with their career better. Less number of hours of work naturally means less income and thus there is a decided difference between men and women in the income they earn. After career interruptions due to marriage, having a baby and raising a family etc., when they return to work they end up as assistants and technicians and the wage gap in the first year is 33% and even after 20 years, the gap of 7 to 10% continues, reports Lehmen (1953). Loring (1980) says that at entry level there was salary equity in engineering. But after the entry level, men received higher salaries in every field at every level of experience, at every degree level and with every type of employer. Salary depends on the type of industry they are employed, in the kinds of work they do and the academic preparation and advanced training one had to undergo. The median average salary for women was found to be less than that of men by most of the studies. It is also true that women did not opt for advance training or degree work.

Barriers at Work

Inter Personal Barriers

Ott and Reese (1975) suggested that women entering engineering suffered a certain degree of social isolation because of their career choice. Males do not prefer highly qualified, career oriented spouses(Hallender and Shofer (1981), Harrison, Guy and Lutfer(1981) state that women who make non-traditional career choices are also the most likely to have non-traditional ideas for family life. Women have also reported more social isolation from same sex peers than men. Women wished to have a spouse who had a higher degree of career commitment. Hence the trend has been that women planned either to be single and employed full time or married and have children and employed part time.

Situational Barriers

Roby (1972) has identified a number of situational barriers. The most pervasive barrier is'sex discrimination' in general. Freeman (1975) reports that there was less encouragement for female students than for their male counterparts; that there was a general climate of 'maleless' especially in male dominated settings report Bourne and Wiokler (1982). In the engineering college itself, women experience sex discrimination; 78.6% of the students experience sex discrimination from the male students, 37% from male laboratory partners, 30% from male laboratory instructors, and 44% from male faculty according to a study by Horst (1981). 65% of the women interviewed in the study perceived sex discrimination in the field of engineering. A widely shared perception is that sex discrimination in engineering is more than in other fields. Sexual discrimination was both overt and covert. Overt behaviour included open statements or behaviour which downgrade one's abilities, aspirations and interests because of one's sex. Covert behaviour included unspoken or subtle negative assumptions about one's abilities, aspirations or interests based on one's sex. A substantial significant proportion of women reported sexual harassment from both male faculty and students. Sexual harassment included unwanted comments, sexual suggestions, sexual advances which puts one in an uncomfortable position.

Indian women engineers have not reported any overt sexual harassment. But some have reported subtle sexual discrimination. Chaturvedi (1985) states that the women engineers had sexual discrimination more from the bosses of their own sex than from male bosses. Women bosses were more strict and authoritative than the men bosses who were understanding and considerate. Women engineers in India faced difficulties working outdoors, supervising construction work specially in villages. They faced conveyance difficulties; they could not go in two-wheelers wearing a sari and villagers did not approve of their wearing pants during supervision; they could not travel late hours; travelling with men colleagues was frowned upon by family members. Women engineers also found it difficult to extract work from male subordinates (Lober 1984) and manage the contractors. Very few women took part in activities connected with the Professional Associations. (Venkatratnam (1971) and Lober (1984). Thus their visibility was very low and this was one of the reasons for their not climbing the social and professional ladder.

Constraints at Home

With a demanding job, full of keen competition, women engineers face role over load and role conflict. Professional role expectations are not congruent with feminine role expectations. Marriage is very important in the lives of Indian women. It is true that women professionals are in great demand in the marriage market to-day due to their potential for earning and prestige of the profession. Most of the women engineers in India tend to get married to men from the same profession or equal professional status. Arranged marriages and dowry practices are common though there is less of dowry giving among women engineers. Women engineers or Physicians, they consider family as their prime responsibility and they try to manage their homes with the help of hired servants or family members. They do feel guilty of neglecting their homes and children. The family career conflicts among all working women is a world wide phenomenon. Women engineers, because of these dual career problems, choose jobs which are not too demanding, with regular working hours, less travelling etc. and consequently end up in lower prestige work, earning less salary.

Attitudes of Women Engineers

The adjectives for women engineers which got the highest ranks are—reliable, independent, adaptable and aggressive in a study by Horst (1982). The trend seems to be that women engineers in USA, with their high intellectual ability, high energy, high motivation and extreme independence are competing successfully with their male counterparts. Among all professionals, women engineers give more support for'feminism' They are more optimistic in their belief in equal pay for equal work. They have more egalitarian relationship with men, more liberal in their perception of sex role orientation. There is an increasing level of confidence among women engineers and the growing emphasis seems to be on career rather than family.

Indian women engineers have been found to be positive in their attitude towards equality of sexes, prohibition of dowry, effective enforcement of the laws, concerning prevention of violence against women such as rape, cruelty to widows, child abuse, prostitution etc.

Conclusion

In the course of the last 40 years, there has been a dramatic change in the attitude of the people in allowing girls to take up professions like Engineering. In India, in 1951 there were hardly 19 girl students in the Engineeering faculty and to-day there are more than 12000 women enrolled in engineering institutions. It is the same in the other countries as well. More and more middle income families are taking advantage of professional education and this is a means of upward social mobility. More women are interested in combining employment with marital and family commitments as 'two pay cheque family' becomes the norm. A large number of women are entering the so called non- traditional careers and engineering seems as a prototype for all traditionally male professions. Many situational barriers and inter personal barriers have been identified and all studies document the pervasive nature of discrimination against women in several settings. But studies have also noted the increasing level of confidence among the women engineers and most of the women are there because of the satisfaction they derive and the sense of achievement they get out of the work. There is considerable room for professional opportunities and growth if one has the ability. One of the engineering managers made a remark that is a fitting conclusion. He says "I hire brains not gender'. According to Erick Erickson, women have to learn "how to be women and workers, wives and colleagues, mother and creative beings and have a sense of continuity'. Engineering and science is well removed from workers' sex differences.

References

Benedicta Pinto A.C., Women Power-Technical Education and Development New Delhi, Classical Publishing Company, 1993

Bernard Jessie., Academic Women, University park: Penn State University Press, 1964

Bernard Jessie, The Female World, Ny., The Free Press 1981

Blau Judith, R., Expertise and power in professional organisation, sociology of work and occupations 6 : 103-23, 1979.

Chakravarthy, R. The status of Women Scientists in India, New Delhi, National Institute of Science, Technology and Development Studies, 1984

Dass Dayal., Development of Technical Education in India, CSL Services, New Delhi, Ministry of Education and Culture, 1984

Data Sarita., Technical Education of Women: an assessment, Bombay, SNDT University, 1984

Davis Nancy.,J.and Lauz Bumpass, The Continuation of Education after marriage among women in the United States, Demography 13 : 161-74 1976

Gandhi Indira., Women Engineer and Scientists, Faridabad, Government of

India Press, 1981

Horst Leslie., Ph.D., Informal Barrier to Women entering Engineers; Cambridge, M.A., Henry Murray Research Center, 1981.

Hill. W.Scott., Women Engineer in Indusiry in women and the Scientific profession ed. Jacquelyn Mott field and Carrolven Aken, Cambridge, MA MIJ Press, 1965

Jaiswal R.P., Status of Working men and women Engineers, unpublished M.Phil Dissertation, Jawaharlal Nehru University, New Delhi, 1956

Joshi. S., Civil Engineering in Seminar on Careers for Women, All India Women's Conference, New Delhi AIWC 1956, pp 81-83

Kalbagh.C.Ed., Women in Enterprise and profession, Discovery Publishing House, New Delhi, 1992.

Kanter, R.M., Men and Women of the Corporation, Ny. Basic Books, Inc.1977

Kala Rani- Role conflict in Working Women, New Delhi, Chiltena Publishers 1976

Khushalani. J.K., Engineering in Seminar on Carrers for Women, Papers and proceedings by AIWC, New Delhi, 1956,pp.84-87

Kundsin Ruth., Women and Success; The Anatomy of Achievement, Ny, William Morrow and Co., 1974

Lemkau Jeanne. P., Personality and background Characteristics of Women in male dominated occupations, a review, psychology of women quarterly 4: 221-40,1979

Michael Jean, Women in Engineering Education, UNESCO, Paris, 1988

Pernell. R.B., Training for professions and careers, National Council of Women in India, Bombay, 1967 pp.175-179

Robin Stanley S., The Female in Engineering in The Professional Woman ed., Athenia Theodore Cambridge MA, Schenkman, 1971

Roby Pamela, Women in the Work Place, Cambridge MA., Schenkman, 1981

Roby Pamela, ed. Child Care: Who Cares? Ny, Basic Books, 1973

Rossi Alice., Barriers to the Career Choice of Engineering, Medicines or Science among American Women in Women and the Scientific Profession Cambridge, MA., The MIT Press, 1965

Silverstone Rosalie and Ward Audrey., ed. Careers of Professional Women, London, Croom Helm 1980

Spencer Anne and Podmone David., ed. In a man's World: Essays on Women in Male dominated profession London, Tavistock Publication, 1987

Sinha Pushpa, Role Conflict among the working women, New Delhi, Ammol Publications 1987

Srivastava A.K., Social Class and family life in India, Allahabad, Chugh publication, 1986

Tangri. S.S., Determinants of occupational role innovation among college women, Journal of Social Issues 28 : 177-184, 1972

US Department of Labour, Bureau of Labour Statistics Washington D.C. 1975-1985

US Women's Bureau, Department of Labour, Hand books 1975-1985

Women Engineers., EITB initiatives, Engineering Industry Training Board, Watford, 1987.

Women Lawyers

Introduction

What women are, what they want and what they ought to do and be are now questions in the minds of many people. Few women are to be found among the ranks of professionals in medicine, engineering, law and sciences and among the managers of industry. Generally people occupying such positions are the manipulators of symbols and power. Over the past decade, more and more women have chosen and fought to enter these spheres and they are demonstrating competence in many fields that were exclusively male domains before.

Should women become lawyers? Does it matter? The answer is it does. Not only is the entry of women into legal profession an important indication of their equality, it also'constitutes a broadening of the professional responsiveness to the needs of all sections of society". Law is one of the most admired professions and high in social rank. Law provides access to important positions in business, government and politics. Poor participation of women in politics and business is most probably due to the small percentage of women lawyers. 'Members of the legal elite preside over power and property relationships; play a leading role in legislative bodies that write tha law: they direct the executive agencies responsible for enforcing the law; they rule the courts that apply the law; they gude the corporate and financial institutions that constitute the most important property interest'. (Epstein 1981).

In the Vedas, we find discussions on the profession of lawyers and Brahma Jayasutra says "law alone is the protector" of society. Lawyers have always received respect from those who count in society. They are the soldiers of peace and prosperity.

With economic liberalization poliicies all over the world and growth of capitalist enterprises, government rules and regulations linked to it have grown complex and incomprehensible to the common man. Specialists are required to interpret the rules and regulations and to guide the institutions in their procedures. Thus lawyers become indispensable in the modern world.

Lawyers function not only as advisers but many of them are

prominent as executive of corporations and as members of boards of directors. Lawyers are very much part of politics and government. In India most members of the parliament and legislative assemblies are lawyers. In the United States, 75% of the senators are lawyers. Representatives and governors are likely to have been lawyers. Many Presidents have been lawyers.

In the 19th century, British laws prohibited women from entering the bar in England and in India. Nevertheless, in 1892, a Parsi Christian, Cornelia Sorabji studied for Bachelor of civil law at Oxford and became the first Indian woman to earn a law degree. She was appointed as a legal advisor to women's court of wards in Calcutta. In response to agitation by women, the government of India passed the legal practitioners (women) Act in 1923, removing the ban on women practising law. There used to be four kinds of legal practitioners- the baristers were the England trained lawyers, vakils were the Indian law college graduates, solicitors were the ones who prepared the brief and advocates were the lawyers who represented in court. Now there is only one class of legal practitioners.

The few women who obtained law degrees did not practise. Of the lawyers listed, only 10% were born before 1920.

As soon as India attained independence, the government planned to create a democratic, just and prosperous society through constitutional and legal reforms. The preamble to the constitution of India resolved to secure to all its citizen, social, economic and political justice, liberty of thought, expression, belief, faith and worship, equality of status and opportunities, dignity of the individual and the unity of the nation. To attain these national objectives, the constitution guarantees certain fundamental rights and freedom such as freedom of speech, protection of life and freedom and personal liberty and prohibition of discrimination or denial of equal protection. Indian women are the beneficiaries of these rights in the same manner as Indian men. Article 14 ensures equality before law; article 15 prohibits any discrimination and empowers the State to make special provision for women. Article 16 guarantees equality of opportunity for all citizens in matters relating to employment or appointment to any office under the State on the grounds of religion, race, caste, sex, descent, place of brith or residence.

Independent India has relied heavily on legislaltion in its effort to usher in a society where there will be no discrimination or inequality. It has emphasised the principle of equality between sexes and in removing all legal discrimination. But legislation by itself cannot change society. Translating the rights into reality is the task of other agencies. Under the Advocates Act, lawyers are not discriminated on the basis of sex. A lawyer is not supposed to have any sex label. He or she is a lawyer first and lawyer last.

In 1950-51, the number of women who had enrolled in law colleges was 290; in relation to men, just 2 females per 100 males joined law colleges. In the next 20 years, i.e. by 1970-71 the total number of females in law colleges was 2626; i.e. per 100 males, 3.7 women joined law colleges. Though the number of women enrolled in law colleges has been on the increase, more than half of them do not practice law. During the seventies only 8 women were appointed to the High court. One out of the 350 High court judges was a woman. According to 1971 census, there were 1700 women lawyers. According to 1988 figures, women practicing law were only 8.5%

The trend is the same in the other countries also: In the U.S., women in law schools rose from 4% in 1960 to 8% in 1970 and then to 33% by 1980s. But the percentage of women practising law which was 1.1% in 1910. rose to 3.5% in 1950, 4.7% in 1970 ,12% in 1980 and it is reported that though 40% of the students who enter law schools are women to-day, half of them do not practice law. In the US during the beginning of this century, women who trickled into the legal profession met considerable resistance from the professional gate keepers. The legal profession was cautious in protecting its reputation and monopoly on its services by limiting the number of practitioners admitted to practice. During the sixties explosive changes in the society occurred; there was an increasing demand for legal services by a growing economy during the sixties and seventies triggered by the expansion of major corporations and there was a quantum jump in the entrance to law schools. The movements of the 1960s were important in pressing for egalitarianism in all spheres. During the sixties anti-discrimination laws to protect women and minorities were passed. The seventies was a decade of legislation and litigation for the rights of women. The civil rights Act of 1964, its amendment in 1972, legal sanction of equal pay for equal work in 1979 etc. were important land marks. In the seventies, barriers to women's legal education were lifted; more and more women looked to law careers as a way of acquiring competence and effectiveness. Law became a mechanism for change as it was implemented by the concerted action of women's movement activities and feminist lawyers. Legal methods were accepted as effective tools for winning women's entry into the male dominated establishments. Political and legal pressures, and liberalised social attitudes led to the increase in proportion of women entering the professions.

Who are the women lawyers? What back grounds do they come from? What influences have shaped them? What occupational heritage do they have? What is the social origin of these lawyers? What are the social, cultural and psychological factors which are responsible for women's choice of law as a profession? What factors were supportive during the training and implementation phases of their career development? What effect does occupational role have on the personal lives of the women lawyers? What are the problems attendant to traditional female roles? What are the stresses between one's work and home? Are there conditions which account for the career success of women lawyers? What is the attitude of women lawyers to the women's issues? What are their contributions to the cause of women?

Studies on women lawyers in India by Chaudhary P. (1973), Gore N.S (1967), Mukherji T. (1960), Sarkar L.(1973), Pahwa K.(1964), Parnell P.B. (1967) Panandikar (1966), Shahai (1976) and on women lawyers in U.S.A. by Barnes (1979), Bysiewieg (1973), Epstein (1981) Ginsberg (1978), Griffin (1970), Super (1959) and White (1967) have been reviewed to gain an understanding of the factors that enable women to enter the male dominated, atypical profession of law, the socio-cultural variables that have an impact on the career choice process, the influence of educational values in the home, significant role models, the effect of the occupational role on the personal lives of women, problems attendant to the traditional female roles and the contribution of women lawyers to the society.

Socio Cultural Background

With roots in tradition and History, Law was generally a worthy profession for the sons of the rich and aratocratic families. The economically comfortable, intellectually talented and the aspiring males joined law colleges. The girls who joined law colleges during the fifties and sixties were from urban upper middle class high income families with well educated parents; about 30 to 40% of the law students, both male and female, had lawyer fathers, which was the strongest single predictor for the choice of law. Fathers were the strong role models.

During the fifties and sixties, there was male hostility towards women students, including the professors in the U.S. reports Stevens (1972). The history of discriminatory practices by the legal profession during the fifties and sixties is well documented in the United States.

In India, more women joined law colleges during the seventies. An interview with women lawyers by Chaudhary(1973) has listed that women joined the legal profession in preference to other professions because - some belonged to lawyer families; for some others, it was a challenging, prosperous and dignified profession where one can have ample opportunities to rise by one's own calibre; and for few others, this profession could help in protecting the rights of the down-trodden workers. All the women lawyers interviewed were of the opinion that it was not meant for men only but what is needed for the legal profession is a critical brain, sincerity, capacity for hard work and ability to concentrate and women are not lacking in any of these. In the profession, all the women lawyers reported that they get on with their men colleagues very well, men are as cooperative and nice as any women lawyer could be and if one could assert one's ability and equality, one is accepted. We do not find any sex discrimination as much among colleagues.

Some felt that if women were successful, it was affiliated to other reasons such as social influence, feminine charm and not to her intelligence. Regarding client relationship, it reported that initially, the clients hesitate to go to a woman lawyer but once they develop confidence in the lawyer — whether man or woman — they go back to the same lawyer. The women lawyers interviewed were Urmila Kapoor, Usha Mehra, Chander Kohli, Padma Jain, Asha Goel, Urmila Nayar and soni Deshpande.

But many women lawyers did not take to practicing law. Women did not favour going into the court rooms and argue. They favoured government work because of the security it provided. They took more of advisors' jobs in banks and trusts; some times they took to small private practices with partnership with family members.

During the eighties we find many women lawyers in low

ranking specialities, unremunerative and so unattractive to males such as matrimonial and family law practices, legal-aid work, child care cases, probate cases etc. But women lawyers' contribution in public interest work representing the poor, aged, disadvantaged, minority women, prisoners, tenants etc. is commendable.

In the beginning, the public — both men and women did not have confidence in women lawyers and they did not bring even their ordinary problems involving civil action, real estate etc. to women lawyers. The women lawyers were also reluctant and ambivalent about getting into the rat-race of getting into business and making money.

Women did go into teaching in law colleges but very few women reached the top as professors or deans of legal studies or principals of law colleges. To-day law is an over crowded profession; many drop out; women do face prejudices in practicing law. A few women do practice law independently. There is a small but growing number of women partnership in already established firms. In judicial positions, not many have climbed to the top. At the level of judges, sub-judges and magistrates, for every 40 men, there is just one woman — according to the figures for 1991 — in the legislative assembly, the proportion is 1:18.

Women lawyers have been active in amending laws of succession rights, laws of property rights, laws of maintenance rights, marriage rights, dowry prohibition, maternity benefits equal remuneration Act, suppression of immoral traffic and girls Act etc. They have also been helping in conducting legal aid camps, legal literacy programmes, legal counselling, protecting rape victims, battered wives and dowry death cases. They have accomplished powerful changes in the rights of women. Law reforms have had impact on middle class urban women but did not penetrate into rural areas.

Women lawyers' association did operate in a limited way as a pressure group to improve the opportunities for women in law. Women Lawyers Association has been persuading voluntary organisations such as All India Women's Conference to provide legal aid to women who had been deserted, widowed and divorced. Women lawyers participated in media campaigns to raise women's awareness on legal rights. All India Women Lawyers',Association hold conferences, and celebrate women lawyers'day by organising national conventions. They have been active in trying to enact a uniform civil code which will neither be Hindu nor Muslim nor Christian but an eclectic collection of all that is good and commendable in many systems. According to them, this is the only way to correct the distortions and promoting equality of sexes and equality of opportunity amongst all citizens irrespective of their religion, region or sex.

Studies on women lawyers in U.S. state that the socio economic background of women entering law schools is the same as in India-from high income families, with educated parents and 35% of law students were from lawyers families. During the sixties women lawyers married and joined their husbands in practice.

During the seventies due to the influence of women's Rights Committee, National Conference of Law Women, Young Lawyers Association etc., women and Law became an accepted course in law schools. Initially, the law firms fid not desire to recruit women or minorities from rural background and those with fathers in blue collar occupations. Women with modest background and who graduated from law schools used to favour government work and as they did not have the proper connections, could not join law firms, they took up the law ranking specialities such as family law, matrimonial low, legal aid, child custody cases and used to assist in routine case preparations.

Feminist law firms and feminist law practice started during the seventies to serve women clients, and other public interest work. A few women did turn out to be successful lawyers such as Ruth Ginsberg, Oliver Wandell, Louis Brandeis and Felix Frankfutter and they did become judges. During the eighties, more women came forward to litigation work, corporate work, labour relations and business law.

To-day a Wall Street lawyer may well be a woman. There are more than 600 women in 3 dozen select firms clustered along the elegant mid town sections of Park and Madison Avenues.

In the social context of egalitarianism, with enormous growth in size in the firms during the eighties, there was need for greater number of recruits; the firms competed to get the best law graduates and more women entered the firms. New legal business was created by the new statutes and regulations dealing with ecology, pollution, consumer affairs, human rights etc. The shape of the profession also changed, from solo practice to corporations and the average net income of lawyers in these firms sky rocketted. A business man, small or large cannot function without an attorney. The number of women partners in New York firms has increased from one woman in 1956 to 29 in 1977 and 41 in 1980. Even to-day some of the largest firms like Sullivan and Cromwell do not have women partners . A survey by the National Law Journal, in 1992 showed that though white males continued to dominate at the powerful and lucrative partnership level of the largest law firms, number of women was rising at all levels. Of the 10 large cities surveyed,. San - Francisco ranked highest with 33% of female lawyers as partners and associates and Boston had 30%. Jobs of law professors have been plums kept from the reach of most women. But women staff in law colleges have increased from 2.2% in 1970 to 10% in 1980. In the past decade. men have relaxed their hold on legal profession permitting women to enter but they have not released their hold.

Not many women join the professional associations like the American Bar Association nor do they attend meetings regularly or elected to offices or decision making bodies. The membership of the National Association of Women Lawyers is only 1600, a mere 2% of American women lawyers.

Studies have found that women have lower self images than men. The self esteem of male law students was found to be higher than that of female students. Different socialization processes probably make for different modes of personality.

The problem of integrating private life and public life continues in the U.S. A common view of career women has been "active lawyers have unhappy marriages".

Studies also report that women lawyers in the U.S. are less likely to be married, if married, less likely to remain married, with divorce rate being high among women lawyers. The recent trend is lawyers are marrying lawyers for companionship as well as support needed to do well in careers. But sometimes a man may well be irritated and diminished by his. wife's success and rank disparity also affects private life. Slims (1982) did a poll on attitudes of woman lawyers towards issues relating to women and found that 4 out of 5 women felt that children were not essential for a full and happy marriage.

There is very little data or case studies available on Indian women lawyers, about their career development, career advancement and constraints faced. According to an opinion poll, most of the women lawyers are under employed, very few actively practice law, they are not very serious on career advancement, almost all of them are happily married to highly educated husbands, and have fewer children than the average families. Several women interviewed said that they completed their law degrees after marriage, with the support of their husbands. They have been able to combine a career with home and children as they get special support of their family network. There were no serious conflicts between family responsibilities and career.

Conclusion

Women have proved their talent for understanding and practising law. Women lawyers, no matter what their family situation or preference of practice, feel that they are capable of matching the men in their profession in ambition, interest, intellectual competence, legal abilities and pursuit of excellence. The disappearance of stereotypes that define women as unlikely professional partners will decide women in future position in the legal world. The barriers once impenetrable has now been broken through but for those who strive to be at the top, the climb is not easy.

Women have encouraged and supported the entrance of other women into law schools and the judiciary; they have called for reinterpretation of the law and its practice; those who entered public interest and feminist practices have accomplished powerful changes in issues of equality in marriage and divorce, equality of employment, protection of victims of physical assault of rape and access to credit.

There is a general feeling that the legal profession has become the servant of the 'haves' rather than the guardians of the 'have nots'; that the ranks of the socially conscious have diminished. It is hoped that women lawyers would work with certian idealism, humanity and with a sense of fairness, objectivity and vision.

References

Chaudhary Pawan., Wome Lawyers in a man's world, Social Welfare V 19(12) 1993, p.p 26-27

Epstein Cynthia F., Women's in law, Ny Basic Books, 1981

Epstein Cynthia F., Women's place: option and Limits in professional careers, Berkeley, University of Californa Press, 1970

Ginsberg Ruth, 'Women's Right to full participation in shaping Society's Course' in Towards the Second Decade, ed. Betty Justice and Renati Pora, Connecticut, Greenwood Press, 1981

Mukherji Tapati, Women's role in dispensing justice, Social Welfare V 7(5) 1960 pp.13-14

Sarkar Lotika., In Law, Seminar No.165, 1973, pp. 13-15

Scott Turow- One L, Cambridge, M.A., Harvard University Press

Simpson G., The daughters of Charlotte Ray:

The Career development process during the exploratory and establishment Stage of Black Women attorneys, 1978, Henry Murray Research Centre, Cambridge MA

U S Bureau of Census.

WOMEN MANAGERS

Nancy Adler and Dofran Izraeli in their book 'Women in Management world wide' (1988) pronounce that although women constitute over fifty per cent of the world's population, in no country, do they represent half or even close to half of the corporate managers. Reasons for the paucity of women in management are fairly similar world wide. Cultural sanctions, educational barriers, legal restrictions, corporate obstacles and women's disinterest in pursuing managerial careers may be listed as the dominant constraints but the relative importance of each varies from one country to another. For example, women in Japan and Saudi Arabia may focus on cultural patterns whereas the American Women may blame the legal structure; Chinese women in Singapore and China may emphasise the current economic conditions and political leadership as the important constraints which have prevented women's representation in management.

G.L. Symons reviewed three cultural settings, namely France, Quebec and English Canada and reported that women's career in business are tempered by blocked mobility, credibility problem and a constant battle against disparaging stereotypes of women as workers who lack commitment and involvement in their occupation.

Audrey Chen from Singapore identifies three factors as responsible for large increase of female managers, namely, economic prosperity, development policies such as changes in university admission criteria and the career aspirations of women. The barriers to career and advancement were the following cultural and social factors - married women were considered unsuitable for jobs that require frequent travel, companies were reluctant to employ women to head a department staffed by men; companies hesitated to employ women to supervising plants, shipyards and construction sites; companies doubted whether married women would take their careers seriously and be willing to work long hours necessary to succeed and employers commonly believed that women would find it difficult to gain the trust and respect of the customers. Singaporean women managers encounter male discomfort, resistance and open hostility from clients, colleagues and subordinates and feel isolated and lonely when they reach top positions.

Because of their upbringing and social pressure, many female managers appear handicapped in the use of direct, overt power; they shy away from major managerial responsibilities and decision making, fail to make straight forward moves to expand their scope of influence and are usually shortsighted in setting their career goals and shaping their career paths. They also have psychological hurdles; they have difficulty in coping with different role expectations and they lack the high power needs and political skills for moving up. A large number feel apologetic about their career commitment and guilty about neglecting child care and family responsibilities and these lead to the limited ambition of female managers.

One in 10 women have been marrying down, since they fail to find compatible marital partners. Women managers in Singapore receive lower salaries than men, with an average of 1313 Singapore dollars as against 2406 Singapore dollars earned by men. Women's Associations in Singapore have been active for eliminating socially indoctrinated sexual bias.

A detailed picture of Singaporean women managers has been given because we find that in almost all the South Asian and South East Asian countries, similar scenario are seen.

Virginia Crockett after studying Indonesia, states that business and management are regarded as male domain; women professional managers hold less visible positions such as office administrators; the invisible ceiling is present for female careers; the society inhibits women's upward mobility, it discourages ego motives, self advancement, individual competitiveness; and mutual aid and collective achievement is the standard. But over the past decade, there is an increasing pool of educated women and due to the influence of western cultural values and the demand of women's organisations for changes in marriage law, education, health and employment issues, more women are filling the executive vacancies in business management. But unless constraints like marriage and motherhood and the negative stereotypes of female managers are removed, women will not be able to reach the top.

Patricia Steinhoff and Tanaka, in their articles 'women managers in Japan', confirm some of the findings of Audrey Chen on Singaporean women managers, especially, the social and cultural factors, the social pressure and the psychological hurdles which are barriers to career advancement. But Japanese women play a much larger managerial role in small and medium enterprises; more than 25000 women are company presidents whereas large corporations have less than 1% of women managers and employ 1/5th of the labour force. As Japan has had more than a century of universal co-educational primary education, 95% of all young people complete high school and 1/3rd go to higher education; hence there is an enormous pool of well educated women in Japan. Women constitute about 50% of labour force; 90% of Japanese women marry before the age of 35 years, fertility is controlled and there is low illegitimacy rate. The unique managerial culture of working long hours, being available late in the night, strong commitment to company work, all co-workers socializing regularly after work to break down status barriers to achieve consensus oriented decision making etc. are too demanding and it is difficult for married women to meet these demands. Due to the age graded internal promotion in large corporations, it will be a very long time before women can reach the top level of management. In 1986, only 1.6% of the companies had women above the rank of division managers, 4.1% had women upto the level of division managers, 21.6% had women up to section heads and 22.8% had women upto subsection heads. A major mechanism for blocking women from the promotion ladder is to exclude them from transfers to offices far away from their homes. The success of women managers has been in small and medium size enterprises. 99.4% of firms are small or medium size and 75% of all women are employed in such enterprises. Smaller family size, reduced household, women's assurance that they can do men's work and new types of enterprise have led to rapid increase of women presidents in these companies.

A study of Japanese Association of Women Executives in 1986 reports that women managers believed firmly that there was no difference in ability between male and female managers but women were at a disadvantage in the world of business. The manufacturing industries had a negative attitude towards managerial posts for women.

Currently, more opportunities are available for women in large firms also and it is likely to increase in the future especially in the public sector. Cultural pressures are now declining and non working wife is no more a status symbol. Mothers are encouraging their daughters to take careers outside the home, but if the son is a manager, they would like their daughter-in-law to be a non-working wife as a personal support to the husband.

In the rapidly growing and economically dynamic region of the pacific islands, Jean Renshaw interviewed the Fiji women managers and reported that due to descent from mixed racial groups, religious affiliation and beliefs and the values of the chiefly clans, a different kind of early socialization process which instills self confidence, equality among males and females, leadership, responsibility, resourcefulness, honesty etc. have enabled women to have an important role outside the traditional home and family. But the number of women in management positions is less than 1%.

In the Western Europeon countries like Belgium, France, Germany, Netherlands, Portugal, Spain and the United Kingdom, out of 420 companies surveyed fewer than half had ever employed a female manager. 15% of the other half claimed that they would never consider promoting a woman into management. Of the companies surveyed, 8% of the managers in U.K., 9% of the managers in France and 13% of Portugese managers were women. Companies in Netherlands, Germany and Italy reported no women in top management.

In country after country, the proportion of women holding managerial positions fall short of that of men. In some countries, over the last decade, the percentages have increased but in none have they approached equality. The same pattern prevails in western as well as eastern cultures, developed or backward, capitalist or socialist or communist countries.

Most of the respondents of the survey believed that women could manage as effectively as the men in their companies. In entry and middle level, there are sizable number of women but there is scarcity of women at the upper level.

In all the countries surveyed in Western Europe, women managers do not receive the same pay as their male counterparts. In Germany, women's salary is roughly 20% less than men's; income gap increases with the size of the firm. There are socio psychological barriers as well as systemic barriers such as prejudice based on stereotypes, fear and insecurity of women in work places, women being not career minded, lack of ambition among women, sexist job advertisement, not acknowledging career breaks and discrimination in training programmes.

With the influence of Sweden, USA and the UN, Women groups' activism and passing of the Law on Equal Opportunity in 1980, affirmative action programme has been introduced and in the future, there may be many changes in favour of women.

Switzerland is rather conservative in terms of the rights of women and their place in society. It was one of the last countries to grant women the right to vote at the federal level in 1971. One canton still denies women the right to vote on cantonal matters. A number of studies during the seventies found that women were concentrated in the least prestigious occupations and at the lower levels of the organisational and institutional hierarchies. The proportion of women among top managers was about 4% and these women were of higher socio economic origin, had fathers in the same professional level and mothers were in paid employment.

The trend now is 30% of the women managers never marry and around 20% are divorced. 30% of women managers have no children. It is found family life and management are far less compatible for women than for men.

There has been a long tradition of women working out side the house in Great Britain. Valerie Hammond in her paper on 'women in management in Great Britain' (1988), writes that women are an essential part of the labour force and 45% of them participate in work outside the home. 10% work in general management posts and 20% in professional posts. There are many different career paths and entry points. University graduation in any subject enter managerial posts and they come up through promotion, examination and selection procedures. Business degrees have a limited currency. With more women entering university education, now about 41.5% number of women in management careers has increased; but they are concentrated in traditional areas such as hotel and catering, retail distributions, public administration etc. With initiative from the government to encourage opportunities for women to enter public life, women are now entering non-traditional sectors like banking, insurance and manufacturing. More training and development programmes are being offered and some 'women only' programmes have been started by the banking sector and civil service. The Government is also actively encouraging women entrepreneurs. British Institute of Management reports that women in the same positions as men, on an average, are paid less by about 3000 pounds a year at the middle management level. At more senior levels, gap widens to about 10000 pounds. In spite of the equal pay act of 1984, job segregation by sex still exists. But women have a right to return to work after child birth after an entitled paid leave of 18 weeks and a further unpaid leave of 11 weeks. Enlightened employers are designing employment options to enable women to combine a family and a career.

In Israel, the policies are midway between Europeon and Middle Eastern countries. The main thrust is concern for the women's role as mother and housewife. High marriage rate, low divorce rate, low birth rate, high commitment to family life are some of the social features. There is a growing awareness among women of Israel of the inequity of the division of labour in the family and of discrimination in the labour market. Powerful women's organisation are helping women to become assertive. With more women getting university education, there is a gradual growth in the proportion of women into lower and middle level managerial positions. There has been an increase in proportion of women managers and administrators from 7% in 1973 to 11.3% in 1983. There is indication of delayed marriage and increase in divorce rate of women who want to achieve top positions. With the expansion of professional army after 1947, compulsory military service of three years for men and one and a half years for women have been prescribed and the Golda Meir effect has been that any woman who is competent and strongly motivated can advance to a key position in the economy has been felt.

In South Africa, with elimination of discrimination clauses regardig race and sex in labour legislation, many women are moving into non traditional careers like entrepreneurship. Companies also are willing to invest in their female human resources. Multi-racial women's groups have been established and they are working together to abolish societal and organistional barriers to career growth and to enhance women's quality of life. In 1960, there was only 25% women in the labour force and in 1980 around 33% are working women. 5.5% of all working women are in the four traditionally female occupations, namely, nursing, teaching, sales womanship and clerical. 80% of the black women are in agriculture or as domestic helpers. The Asian women work in small family business. Till recently, the major barrier was the status of married women as legal minors. The matrimonial property act of 1984 endows women with full contractual capacity for white, coloured and Asian but not flor the blacks who are subject to traditional laws. The black women had to get written permission from a male-husband or father or son to enter employment. Acute shortage of supportive facilities, high regard for traditional female roles, lack of training for career development etc., are the factors detrimental to women's advancement in career. The encouraging trend is change—changes in the legal status of women, greater opportunities for girls for education, campaign by women's groups and career aspirations of women.

In Canada and United States, managers are recruited directly from universities. Caroline Andrew Cecille and Ann Denis (1988) in their article on Canadian women managers state that since 1970, the member of women managers has increased substantially from 36% to 54% in 1984. But 30% of the women are still in clerical jobs. In 1971 16% of all managers and 4% of senior managers were women. Ten years later, 25% of all managers and 9% of senior managers were women. The more senior the position, lower the percentage of women.

The profile of women managers is that they came from families of higher levels of education and advantaged background; fathers hold management positions or were professionals; they had employed mothers; they desired to combine family and profession; they had high commitment to work; they were satisfied with their positions, displayed female solidarity and acted as mentors.

In USSR, women's family roles are unchanged despite the fact that they are expected to participate fully in work. As a result, although there are many women doctors and engineers, top positions in these and other fields are primarily held by men. Most organisations would prefer a married man in the top position for he has a support system in his personal as well as his occupational life. Women have never had such double support system as is evident by the often repeated lament of the career women that all she needs is a 'wife'.

In this respect, Sweden, two decades ago, made a bold attempt to change the very nature of society and the role of men and women in the family. The Government made a formal commitment to provide equal employment opportunities and equal participation in family life for both men and women. Paternity leave as well as maternity leave for both parents are available and the husbands are given formal training in child care, thus both men and women in the family are afforded the same practical opportunities of participating in both—active parenthood and gainful employment.

All over Europe, many of the top female executives are with the U.S. companies. Americans' acceptance of women managers is influencing Europeon companies. Seeing the successful performance of American women managers in banks, Britain has been increasingly hiring women for the banks.

In the United States, a number of studies have been done on the various aspects of women in management. There is such a surfeit of facts that the problem is how to synthesize the findings of the studies and make some sense out of it. There are national surveys, analog studies, behavioural studies and some longitudinal studies as well. Studies on managerial climate, managerial models, managerial effectiveness, informal net works for women in management, women's integration into public management, attitude towards working women, career differences among male and female managers, attitudinal barriers to women's aspirations, sex role stereotypes, income differences, career development of the MBA graduates etc. have been conducted by the following scholars -

Bailyn (1974), Barner (1980), Bass (1971), Beck (1980), Bowmen (1965), Diggory (1966), Epstein (1974), Forgarty (1971), Fox (1989), Goldberg (1968), Gordon (1975), Gordon and Stroffer, Guy (1993), Harlan (1976), Hennig and Jardin (1977), Horner (1972), Kanter (1977), Larwood (1977), Lewis and Emmert (1986), Marchiloni (1980), O'leary

(1974), Prather (1971), Rosen and Jorden (1974), Schein (1973), Schulman (1982), Stein (1973), Suter (1973), Tayhor (1974), Wallace (1987) and others and a synthesis of the findings gives us the following picture.

In the United States of America, it had become acceptable for women to fill clerical positions to the public service by 1850. Women stenographers were found capable specially because of their ability to radiate sympathetic interest, agreeableness and courtesy in the office (Kanter 1977). Women came in large numbers into the office in clerical positions during the first half of this century.

Prior to adoption of the 1964 civil rights act, women were systematically excluded from even the entry level managerial positions. In an effort to provide equal opportunities, organisations began a number of changes designed to overcome the barriers that had kept women in the clerical job categories. The equal employment opportunities Act of 1972 brought in changes in policies of recruitment, selection processes, advancement policies and in programmes designed to encourage women's movement into management, and these changes enabled more number of women to enter managerial cadres. According to the Bureau of labour statistics, from 15% in 1964 the proportion of women in management increased to 25% by 1979. In private industry women comprised only 17% in 1980. Despite the increase, women still held low prestige jobs and earned only 55% of which men earned. Sex segregation has been a remarkably stable feature of the American work places all these years. Although the proportion of women and men employed in professional and technical jobs is roughly the same for both sexes, women are employed in traditional female jobs such as health, ,human services, education etc. and the top ranks are invariably filled with men in public management. But there has been rapid progress since the seventies in women's integration into public management. There has been a great impact of equal opportunities initiative of the Government. In 1970, women made up only 1.4% of federal employers in the top grades. By 1985, women composed 6.1% (Fox 1987) at the State leval and at the local levels also, the same trend is seen.

Though a narrowing of wage gap is seen, there is still lack of pay equity between the sexes and women are often relegated to working in less valued mission that pay lower wages. According to Lewis and Emmert (1986) one kind of the male-female earning gap is attributable to occupational sex segregation. Systemic causes, accordidng to Kanter (1977), are the effect of opportunity, power and numbers. Kanter's hypothesis is that women, low in opportunity potential for occupational mobility and growth will react with depressed aspiration, low commitment and non-responsibility. If men and women were in positions of equal opportunity, the behavioural differences would disappear. Kanter sees power as a structural variable and since women have access to so little informal power, they become restrictive of others, risk averse, rulesminded and control oriented. The same was found by Fogarty (1971) and Hansen's survery in 1974.

Kanter also pointed to the role of numbers as a determinant of organisational behaviour. In most organisations, women constitute a highly visible minority. As more visible they are more pressured to perform well, more isolated, more uncomfortable and more excluded from informal net work. Thus the confluence of opportunities, power and proportion produces upward cycles of advantage or downword cycles of disadvantage.

Studying the career differences among male and female managers, Harlan (1976) found that though her sample was essentially similar in terms of marital status, education, work history, area of specialization etc. in the market place, males appeared to be more successful than the females. Several possibilities for the lower success rate for women she identified are, overt discrimination in American business houses, ability differences, remaining single, family obligations and aspirations of the managers. It was found that discrimination was less of a difficulty than it was in the past; there was no ability difference, actually the women tendered to be over achievers as they had the 'I will show them' attitude; remaining single also did not seem to be the answer and it was more the need of their balancing their personal and professional lives which the women felt to be the answer. Many women deliberately chose positions that don't demand too much time or energy. These women had developed internal standards of success that included doing the job well but caring less about attaining external symbols of success such as new levels of responsibility which would take them away from the life style they had. They felt that life was more than an office with 'President' on the door. There has always been an option for a woman to be less career oriented in order to accommodate her husband and family. But for the men however, being successful in a career was synonymous with being a good father and husband.

Gail Schulman (1982) analysing the cultural contradictions the women managers face, says that the business world does not exist in a vacuam, distinct from the rest of the society; it reflects and reinforces societal values and social norms. If equality is to prevail within the business world, not only must corporatations change but so must the societal values which pervade the corporation. Lotte Bailyn (1974) listed three sources which constrain women's work as—the self, the family and the professional world. Epstein (1970) stated that the first experience of discrimination is felt in the early socialisation and dependency training. Boys are raised more permissive than girls and are allowed to display more aggression and autonomy. Girls are groomed to be personable, compliant and willing to please. So females are at a disadvantage when asked to exhibit autonomy in a leadership situation. Henning and Jordon (1977) say that girls are at a distinct handicap in learning how to work as part of a team as they do not get this experience in the sports field. Thus Bandura's social leaning theory that since parents differentially reinforce appropriate sex role behaviour, boys learn to be dominant and girls to be affiliative is confirmed.

Another psychological approach which offers explanation for the potentially different managerial abilities of men and women is Kohlberg's cognitive development analysis. Maleness connotes cultural ideas of assertion and power and femaleness cannotes cultural ideas of friendliness and accommodation; boys and girls aim to develop different areas of expertise and ability differences are internalized. However, most studies show that men and women have similar intellectual abilities and it is motivation rather than ability which often handicaps potential women managers.

Fogarty, Rapoport and Rapoport (1971) in their study of British University graduates state that even though women do value their careers, they value them some what less than men do. According to Martina Horner, women's achievement strivings are a product not only of the motive to succeed but also of the motive to avoid success. O'Leary (1974) states that the lower self esteem of women aggravates the motive to avoid a task in order to avoid failure. Larwood (1977) adds that over confidence is unbecoming in a female, hence she is handicapped. Marchioni (1980) says that women internalize sex role stereotypes, inhibit their need for achievement and try to pursue only attainable feminine goals. Thus lower expectations cause performance decrements. When such stereotypes are internalized role conflict will follow for any woman aspiring to a managerial position. There are contradictions between images of females and images of managers among women who attempt to enter management.

The second category of barriers to women's career advancement is the family. Here, practical problems, time contraints and role over load become critical. Family demands do detract women from their job commitment and job performance.

Fogarty etal (1971) come to the conclusion that women are far more likely to have continuous work pattern if their careers receive support from their husbands. Such support allows a woman to commit herself to her job without feeling guilty for neglecting her responsibilities in the household.

Wallace (1982) uses the term 'the five year scramble' to describe how the first five years after entering a firm is crucial to prove oneself and women beginning a family during these years, which often happens, are at a great disadvantage as they have to expend a lot of time and energy managing the home front. Thus the demands of the family constitute another reason for not having more women managers at the top.

The third category of barriers consist of those stemming from the professional world. The masculine ethics of bureaucracy, rationality rules and competition so dominate the business world that women are routinely assigned to people- handling job such as personnel department and thus excluded from the main stream of the organisation, says Kanter (1977). There have been a number of studies on this aspect and the consensus of the findings are—stereotype prevails; there is significant similarity between perception of managers. Women would have to develop'male characteristics' to succeed in business organisations. Fogarty's (1971) study showed that men believe women to be 'bad risks' and so they are not accepted as colleagues, superiors or business partners. Many studies have shown that when women succeed in a 'masculine task' the results are attributed to 'luck' but when men succeed, the results are attributed to skill. They conclude that the most prestigious job in the business world, managerial positions,have been sex typed as male, while the least prestigious jobs, the clerical positions have been sex typed as female.

Even when women eventually do obtain a managerial position, they are placed in a 'double-bind'. If women emulate masculine qualities, they are considered aggressive and unfeminine; if they exhibit sex role appropriate behaviour, they are considered unsuitable for the job and are not taken seriously. Praether (1971) explains that a good looking woman is seen as frivolous and incompetent and the not so good looking is seen as aberrant. If a woman manager is married, the assumption is that for her, the family is more important than her job; if not married, she is considered as not being serious about the job. If women object to dirty jokes in informal conversation, she is supposed to be lacking in sense of humour; if she shares the dirty jokes, it is considered a mark of incompetence. The result is that women seldom know what type of behaviour to display. They must prove themselves as competent despite their sex, yet must not destroy men's notions about appropriate sex role. Kanter (1977) has coined another word 'role encapsulation' to describe the process by which the majority group attempts to make the minority group fit neatly into the appropriate stereotypes. For example, men attempt to interact with women in terms of one of the four clearly defined social roles — mother, seductresspet or an iron maiden. Mother is a sympathetic listener, seductress is in the sense when one concentrates her attention on one man and risks debasement if she shares her attention widely; pet for a cute amusing mascot expected to admire male displays of competence and iron maiden for a tough, dangerous, militant feminist. All these limit a woman's ability to be effective within an organisation.

The sex typing of managerial roles as masculine is perhaps the most important factor responsible for the problems women face in business settings (Bowman etal 1965, Epstein 1970, Orth 1971, Short 1974).

Women are usually excluded from the informal activities in corporate life; they are denied access to the informal net work of the corporation. Generally,business is transacted to a great extent,in informal settings, such as clubs or golf course where contacts are made, friendships are forged, wheels are greased and new talent recruited', Women are usually made to feel unwelcome for such informal discussions. Beck (1980) says that nearly two dozens of the most prestigious business clubs across the country still don't grant membership in their own rights. In some clubs, women have different entrances to the facilities and dine in separate rooms. Late night business dinners are held in clubs without inviting women managers. The protege system exemplifies the exclusion of women. Most executives are men and they dare not sponsor a woman, however efficient she might be, for fear of their wives' jealousy. Therefore women lose access to information, contacts and privileges accorded to such proteges. A mentor acts as a teacher, sponsor, host and guide, who provides moral support to his protege. Finding a true mentor relationship is tragically a rare observance for women (Fury, 1980).

Women lack system knowledge or understanding of the ins and outs of the fringe benefits and perquisites because they more often lack well connected peers or sponsors who would make informal introduction or educate them about the real working of the system. It is not what you know but who you know continues to hold true for women who want to get ahead. Who to contact for information, whose support to seek for what purpose etc. are as important as knowing the job. Network is the connections that help the members by providing support, information and business opportunities. Few women are accepted automatically into the elite network of the corporation; they are usually'uninformed' do not know the ropes' or 'lack clout'; they are not in a position to take the kind of risks that build credibility.

The practice of 'fast tracking ie. identifying the top management candidates early in their careers and grooming them creates many dilemmas for women who wish to move up the corporate ladder as criteria for this selection includes appearance. presentability, family standing, social background, professional membership, sports and recreational activities and the acquisition of the attitudes, values and behaviour patterns of successful superiors who are almost always males.

Corporate gamesmanship ie. non recognition of the hidden political processes of the organisation can be detrimental to a woman's progress.

Sexuality as a factor enters into the picture in a variety of ways ranging from the more serious to less significant. Inequality in gaining entry into informal group for work enhancement due to sex is one of the toughest to remedy (Strober and Cordon 1978).

To the question do male and female managers differ from each other, the findings of the innumerable studies have been contradictory and inconclusive. Some of the major findings are female managers tend to be less competitive than males in their work; they are likely to adopt an informal and personal style of work; they tend to have horizontal rather than vertical ambition; women are more likely to be conscientious over details than men; they are disinclined to delegate power and perform better at routine tasks than at initiating new plans. Women value friendship on the job as an end in itself where as men see it only as a means to greater success; female managers are risk averse than male managers. Women focus on planning and achieving current tasks where as men focus on long term goals; women see their careers and their lives as distinct and they attempt to keep the two separate; they view jobs in terms of personal growth, self fulfilment and a contribution to others, whereas men value success, hierarchy of power and health; they have vertical ambitions, they like to compete, take risks, set long term goals, initiate new plans and identify themselves with work and organisation. They define career as a progression of jobs leading upward to recognition and reward.

Their lives centered around work, their families were potential sources of support and symbol of their success; growth is an intrapsychic development rather than an interpersonal one. As women have less self confidence, and less time to devote to work, such a success pattern seem a difficult goal.

Rosaline Loring and Thendoran Wells(1982) describe the type of managerial climate which would be most adaptive to moving women into management. The more acceptance of women as individuals, as people, the more egalitarian the climate. The more egalitarian the climate, the more likely will women be found participating in a wide range of positions at management decision making levels. To comply with new laws, the top management should implement the affirmative action programme for women and it has to be authoritative in order to accomplish rapid behavioural change.

The degree of 'Masters in Business Administration' has often been assumed as the key to managerial opportunities and a passport to managerial success for both men and women. The number of women in MBA classes rose meteorically during the seventies and eighties. Several longitudinal studies on male and female MBAs and their career advancement show that male MBAs were substantially ahead of women MBAs in career success and earnings. The salary and responsibility gap appeared to widen over time so that 10 to 15 years post MBA, women were earning only 59% of what their male counterparts earned and were at much lower levels in the organizational hierarchy. The issue for women managers no longer appears to be entry. Most corporations have made great strides in identifying and breaking down barriers that prevent entry into management. A greater challenge is identifying and eliminating barriers that prevent women's advancement in management. The psychological barriers and the organisational barriers have already been discussed. The trends and future implications of all these studies and their findings are—men and women are available in infinite variety; women are making advances into management posts; socialization processes are changing. Changes are noticed in masculine stereotypes, The younger people are becoming liberated husbands sharing home making and child care responsibilities; Sex discrimination is expected to die a natural death in the next ten to fifteen years; The impact of women's changing roles is potentially greater than all the advances in science and technology; Percentage of women in supervisory, professional, managerial and executive positions will increase dramatically; Organizations would respond more readily to society's changing value system; The strategies needed for integrating demand with productivity are : make sponsorship a requirement, affirmative action an 'in' project, recruit the best possible women, give them the same accoutrements as to men, engender a climate of social approval of women managers, provide supplementary training, incorporate flexi time and job sharing opportunities and improve the general working conditions with child care available, sanctioning maternity as well as paternity leave and offering a cafeteria system of benefits. (Bailyn 1982, Larwood & Gatek 1987).

In India till two decades back, women did not join the Corporate world. Till 1948, there was prohibition against women taking higher Civil Service examination and even when it was ended only unmarried women or widows without encumbrances could join the services. The first woman joined the Indian Administrative Service only in 1951. The first woman joined the Indian Police Service only in 1992. According to the 1991 census, the proportion of women is 6% in all Civil Services, 7.5% in I.A.S and 10% in the foreign services. In the Police Service women has increased from one in 1972 to 21 at present.

As compared to other countries like USA and UK there have been a limited number of studies in India on women in the managerial cadre. A considerable number of consulted papers dealt with women as administrators as executives and entrepreneurs. Consulted research on women executives resorted to self reporting as a prime tool.

Geetha Chaturvedi (1988) in her study on women administrators of India reports that women lag behind that of men with similar initial performance and the barriers to women's advancement are the conflicts between family responsibilities and career commitments, systematic gender inequality and the hidden processes in the organisation. Mehda Dubashi Viz (1987) studied the women entrepreneurs of India and reported that women lacked in self confidence, and the social pressures and society's lack of confidence in women were responsible for women's unwillingness to become entrepreneurs.

Kamala Singh (1992) confirms the above findings and says that lack of confidence in women's ability and male dominance were the main constraints faced by majority of women and women entrepreneurs are unable to make satisfactory progress because of technical, financial and other constraints.

M.J.Louis (1988) in her study on 'women executives of Tamilnadu' interviewed bank executives, doctors, engineers, business women and educationl administrators, all at the executive level and she identified their common problems as social pressures, familial pressures and professional pressures. Guilty feeling of neglecting house hold responsibilities, tension and conflict with family members, lack of support services, lack of opportunities for training, lack of facilities for professional growth etc.have been identified as the factors contributing to the pressures.

Women entered the corporate sector into managerial positions only during the sixties. But they worked only in the area of public relations and labour welfare. In the mainline functions of marketing or finance, there were very few. In the seventies, areas of market research and human resources development saw the entry of women. Banks have been recruiting them, but women managers constitute only 7 to 8% in sharp contrast to employers being 30 to 35% of the work force. The early eighties witnessed an increasing number of women chartered accountants and their induction, for the first time, into the area of industrial relations. Some women joined research and development cells also.

Management in corporate sector is still a male dominated system, especially at the senior levels. Some companies, as a policy, do not employ women; in some others, they are employed only in staff functions. Just a few have them in the policy and decision making levels. Girls opted for professional careers in a big way in the mid eighties and by the end of the decade they were at junior executive levels and now they are in middle management positions. The number of women in these positions will increase in the coming years. By 1995, it is estimated that around 2.5 lakhs of women will be in the banking and financial sectors alone.

A study by Deepti Bhatnagar and Vidya Nair of the Indian Institute of Management reports that although women are recruited in large numbers than before, there continues a bias in allocation of jobs. As women do not get challenging jobs they are not able to prove their worth and move up; they get stuck in the dead end'female' jobs. The organisation cling on to stereotype beliefs such as 'women do not want to travel' 'women prefer secure, low risk jobs etc. and under utilise the potentials of women.

Amba Rao (1979) in her study pointed out that Indian Women lack models and mentors for direction and development. The trend in the nineties, is that women are making their marks in production function and general management. Women seem to be more comfortable in Hi-tech business environments in the electronics and computor software industries.

Though more and more avenues have opened to women at all levels, a very small proportion of these reach the top rungs. The concern of many of the scholars in the nineties have been on this question—what is it that keeps women managers from reaching the top despite good qualifications, good opportunities and women's high motivation to pursue a career? National Conferences were organised in 1988 in New Delhi, in 1989 in Bombay and in 1990 in Madras by the All India Management Association and the issues of managerial effectiveness of women, career development and the challenges and constraints they face have been discussed and deliberated. One encouraging finding pointed out in one of the conferences was that the growth rate of women in the banking and finance profession as a whole was faster than that of men. Between 1960 and

1980, recruitment of women officers has risen from 25% to 68%, women staff from 34% to 53% and women sub staff from 12% to 50%.

Some of the desirable qualities that women managers should adhere to in order to be successful were identified as — effectiveness in practice and keeping away from group politics; improvement of general knowledge; keeping abreast of the latest developments in their chosen fields; acceptance of line jobs; development of options and inter changeability in career and attendance in all office parties and socialising since much useful information and knowledge can be gleaned through these informal channels.

Punam Sehgal (1992) in her article on 'women managers coping with challenges' makes an interesting statement that the laws legislate equal opportunities but they cannot legislate equal access to these opportunities and they cannot ensure that people who have been traditionally descriminated against will immediately take advantage of the opportunities.

The socialisation process, the stereotyping of the achieving male and nurturant female, the conflict between the managerial role expectations and feminine role expectations, resentment by male collagues in the work place, isolation and hence high visibility of women managers, the 'queenbee syndrome'of some women managers, lack of role models, mentors and net working among the women, the managerial politics and power game, organisational pressure and familial pressure, attempting to be a super woman — all these factors which have already been discussed in detail with reference to the other countries are all true for India also.

It is also true that women are establishing themselves as a strong presence in the upper echelons of the corporate sector but they are still a minority.

In 'Femina' of 23rd January 1993, Ramya Sarma has put together interviews done at Madras, Bangalore, Calcutta, Hyderabad and Delhi in her article, `Cindrellas in the Board room'. Following are the highlights of some of the findings.

"The scene is changing in the corporate world" Christine Fernandes (1993) the general manager, Taj, Bangalore states; she continues, the male is no longer the automatically superior being just as woman is no longer forced to fight for equality on a gender basis. Her brain is no longer judged on par with his brain, her beauty is rarely the deciding factor. He is no longer better just because he is male— in fact he is unsuitable for a job that optimally requires the "womanly" attributes of patience, sensibility, intitution and persistance". She feels that women are better managers as they are more sensitive and correct in their judgement as they consider the individual and person being judged rather than just the fact. Women would make better managers with their ability to communicate, harmoniously work with others and to initiate, innovate and lead. Women in their thirties now, are unaware of any discrimination on sexual bias.

Vinite Dang, the advertising manager, Proctor and Gamble says that she has never encountered chauvinism or discrimination in her ten years of experience in the corporate field. She feels that if you come through as firm, clear, balanced, a little aggressive (better termed as assertive, perhaps) fair and data based, one would not have any adverse reactions from male colleagues.

Rama Bijapurkar, the deputy managing director, Marketing and Research group, also stresses the fact that as she is secure in her abilities she has no problem with the male-female divide. She also feels that unless and until you get full support from your family, especially the husband, it would be difficult to get on in the career.

According to Mahnez Curnelly, communication consultant, Good relations Ltd., success has to be defined according to the individual. Having a stable domestic set up as well as a job which gives her satisfaction, she considers as success for her. She also feels that one has to learn the rules of the game, have to be manipulative if need be, establish your credentials, and with greater sensitivity, endurance, threshold, greater understanding of problems, women managers can function extremely well.

Kamal Printer from Hindu, Bombay office, feels that a version of male chauvinism still pervades corporate life, but a firm business like attitude would help change the general male attitude in the long run.

Chandni Sehgal, the administrative head of Samrat properties, says that there has been a marked change in the corporate scene from 1986 onwards with women coming from I.I.M., I.I.T. and with other foreign degrees women were no more exceptions. She challenges men to handle the home and work the way women do. It would take some time before women get established, to be accepted as female bosses. But in course of time, with a lot of tenacity and tolerence and buidling relationships and net works, women can come up in their careers, "women are the smarter sex", she says.

Tasneem Kidwani, senior officer, HFDC feels that male chauvinism is not totally non-existent; it appears more in home situations than in work situations. The organisation does not distinguish between the sexes but by capabilities, and male clients treat you as they would any man. If they get a sympathetic hearing, they don't even notice that you are a female.

Padma Sinha, manager, planning, in Lakme Ltd., says that there has been a definite change in the past nine years and men are more accepting of women as equals. According to her, most women are, meticulous, sensitive, and responsible and therefore they are better people managers.

Rajan Bala, editor of Gem and Jewllery feels that it may take a while for more women to become bosses but awareness is coming into society that women have a role to play in executive circles.

Mr. Bala subramaniam, Chief executive of B.A.S.F., asserts that in a managerial position, chauvinism does not apply at all. The corporation appoints people for their ability to fill the position and not for their sex. In Times of India, the 28th March 1993, an article by O.P. Malik entitled 'sex on the management mind' talks about the DTE factor, i.e., Drive, Target achievement and Earnestness and how women have the edge in these factors. The opinions of some of the managers, both men and women are given below. Sarita Gandhi, Corporate personnel, Eicher Good earth explains that 'it is the person's competence which matters; gender certainly is no longer the issue! Mr. Ravi Virmani, director, Nohel House confirms the same when he says 'in this increasingly competitive area, employers are looking for a professional. Anybody who can do the job well is being employed'.

Women are more adjusting, sensitive, compliant and this could be an asset in the new concept of participative management, feel many women managers. As women are good at communication, the degree of confrontation is much lower, making them easy to work with.

'Women managers are more patient and more understanding than their male counterparts. Their sincerity index to the job, organisation and their profession is far higher' says Mr. Virmani.

A large number of employers also find women managers more balanced and dedicated with an ability to handle work-related stresses and emotions more efficiently says Malabika Shaw, Deputy Director All India Management Association. She adds 'a women can prioritise tasks faster and is generally more focussed to solving problems'.

Vinayaka Chatterji, Director, Feedback Ventures and Collaborations, says "women managers tend to have more empathy and are more loyal in the context of job hopping".

Haribaskaran, Manager, Citi Bank Cards, says that the male peers and colleagues do not feel threatened enough to feel antagonistic towards women.

Vijay Thadani, Director, NIIT feels that discrimination against women particularly at senior levels is disappearing and if a person is sincere, hardworking, earnest and willing to learn, then gender is irrelevant.

Thus we do find that in to-days's corporate world, professionalism is replacing gender as a criterion for employment and women can look forward to a brighter future in management positions.

References

Adler, N. and Izraeli, D. Women in Management World Wide, M.E.Sharpe Inc, NY, 1988.

Annstead Bette., Women in Management, N.J. Prantice Hall, 1985.

Bailyn, L., "family constraints of women's work", In R.B. Kundsin (ed). *Women and Success : The Anatomy of Achievement* New York: William Morrow and Co., 1974.

Barnes, B., Informal Networks for Women in Management, Murray Centre, 1980.

Bass, B.M., Krussel, J., and Alexander, R.A. Male managers' attitudes toward working women. *American Behaviroal Scientist*, 1971, 15, 221-237.

Bowman. G.W., Worthy, N.B. and Greyser, S.A. Are women executives people? *Harvard Business Review*,, 1965. 43 14-17.

Epstein C.F. Bringing women in: Rewards, punishment, and the structure of achievement. In R.B. Kundsin (ed.). Women and success: *The anatomy of Achievement* New York: William and Morrow and Co., 1974.

Fogarty, M.P., Rapoport., R., and Rapoport, R.N. *Sex Career, and Family* Beverly Hills: Sage Publications, 1971.

Goldberg, P. Are women prejudiced against women? *Trans-Action* , 1968, 5, 28-30.

Gordon, F.E. and Strober, M.H. (eds.), *Bringing Women into Management* New York: Mc Graw-Hill Book Co., 1975.

Harlan, A. Career differences among male and female managers. paper presented at the National Academy of Management, Kansas City, M.O., 1976.

Hofman, L.W. Early childhood experiences and women's achievement motives. Journal of Social Issues, 1972, *28*, 129-155.

Horner, M.S. Toward an understanding of achievement related conflict in women. Journal of Social Issues, 1972, 25 157-176.

Kanter, R.M. Men and women of the Corporation. NY: Basic Books, Inc., 1977.

Larwood, L. and Wood, M.M. *Women in Management*, Lexington, MA: D.C. Heath & Co., 1977.

Loring R. and Well S.T., Break through: Women into Management, Von Nostrand Reinhold Co., 1972.

Marchiloni, B.A. *The psychology of women and the organisation: A literature review.* Unpublished manuscript, October, 1980.

O'Leary, V. Some attitudinal barriers to occupational aspirations in women. Psychological Bulletin, 1974, *81*,809-826.

Prather, J. Why can't women be more like: A summary of the sociopsychological factors hindering women's advancement in the professions. *American Behaviour Scientist.* 1971, 172-182.

Rosen, B., and Jerdee, T.H. Influence of sex role stereotypes on personal decisions. Journal of Applied Psychology, 1974, 59, 9-14.

Schein, V.E. The Relation between sex role stereotypes and requisite management characteristics, *Journal of Applied* Psychology, 1973, *57*, 95-100.

....., The relation between sex role stereotypes and requisite management characteristics among female managers. Journal of Applied Psychology, 1975, *60*, 340-344.

Stein, A.H. and Bailey, M.M. The socialization of achievement motivation in females. *Psychological Bulletin*, 1973, *80*, 345-366.

Suter, L.E. and Miller, H.P. Income differrences between men and career women. *American Journal of Sociology*, 1973, *78*, 962-974.

Taynor, J. and Deaux, K. When women are more deserving than men: Equity, attribution, and perceived sex differences. *Journal of Personality and Social Psychology*, 1974, *29*, 80-85.

Trigg L. and Nerlman, D. Social Influences on Women's pursuit of non-traditional career.*Psychology of women Quarterly*, 1976, 1, 180-189

Wallace. P., Women in the Work Place - Talk given at Radeliffe College, April 23, 1982.

Ambe Rao, The managerial manistream and Indian Women, *Indian management* 18(11) 1979.

Chaturvedi G., Women Administrators in India, Jaipur, R.B.S.A. Publication 1985.

Louis M.J.Women executives of Tamil Nadu, Mother Teresa Women's University, Kodaikanal, 1990.

Malik, O.P., Sex on the management mind, The Times of India Review 28 March 1993.

Pillai J.K. Development and Advancement of Women in Management, un Pusblished paper 1990.

Rai. Usha; Success or Failure in executive position, Social Change V 2, 1972.

Saigal Punam, Women Managers - coping with challenges, *Indian Management*, June 1982

Sankaran, L. Women Executives - To-day's phenomenon and tomorrow's reality, *Integrated Management* V 14 (4) 1979.

Sarma Ramya, Cindrellas in the Board room, Femine, Jan 23, 1993.

Singh, D.R., Women Executives in India, *Management International* Review V 20 (2) 1980.

Singh Kamla, Women Entrepreneurs, Ashist Publishing House, Delhi 1992.

Tewari, H.C. Understanding Personality and Motives of Women Managers, Michigan, UMI Research Press 1980.

Unwallie J.M. ; Beyond the House Hold Walls - A study of women executives at work and at home - Tata Institute of Social Sciences, Bombay 1977.

WOMEN PROFESSIONALS—SUGGESTIONS FOR ADVANCEMENT

According to Erik Erikson, "there is always a historical lag between any emancipation and the inner adjustment of the emancipated; it takes a much longer time to emancipate what goes on deep down inside us-whatever prejudices and inequalities have managed to become part of our impulse life and our identity formation-than the time it takes to define professed values and to change legalities".

If we look at the experiences of women professionals, the world over, we can realise the truth of what Erikson says. The 'agreed upon' research findings on women professionals whether managers or engineers or lawyers or physicians or scientists or architects or enterpreneurs are:-

1. Women lack self confidence; they have low self esteem.

2. Their aspiration level is lower than men's .

3. They lack competitiveness and assertive behaviour.

4. They feel emotional and sensitive to the feelings of others.

5. They feel inadequate and uncomfortable in men's world of work.

6. Their internalized sex role expectation leads to fear of sex role inappropriateness which causes high anxiety, fear of success, avoidance of success and results in lower achievement.

7. Feminine role expectation comes into conflict with professional role expectation and results in a guilt feeling of neglecting family and children.

8. Trying to be a 'superwoman' the burden of dual role responsibilities takes a toll on their mental and physical health.

9. They are unfamiliar with the self presentation game, lacking the necessary clout.

Despite the obvious obstacles, a few women can be seen pursuing the professions and reaching remarkable degrees of success. What is their advice to young women who are ambitious, capable and truly interested in advancing in their careers? The first piece of advice that is given by a successful chrystallographer, Iseabelle L. Karle is 'Never demand equality on the basis of sex without full qualification-it will eventually prove to be a detriment to a complete acceptance of women in the scientific and professional fields'. She says that women should approach their efforts with quiet determination but without belligerence. Quality leads to success in the long run, resulting in a firmly established basis for recognition.

Mildred S.Dresselhands, a successful electrical engineer says that determination, capacity for hardwork, efficiency and positive outlook on life helped her in realizing her professional career. She advises young women to exploit every opportunity that comes one's way, arrange one's personal life so that one can succeed in the professional activities.

One basic advice which all successful women give is that provided one is willing and able to work hard, with self discipline, one can achieve anything one really wants to; acceptance at the top is difficult but achievable.

Ruth Weiner, Chairperson of the department of Chemistry, Florida International University advises young women, 'set high goals for yourself and set them independently of your sex. Be prepared to work hard and don't sacrifice your ambitions, aggressiveness, or intelligence for any of the standard feminine rewards like marriage. If you marry, marry some one in sympathy with your goals. Learn to deal casually with sexism and discrimination; try and ignore them'.

They also advice women to be ready to shift from one job to the other, one field to another. 'Do something more to your liking.Be flexible, be mobile, then you succeed.'

They also suggest that the employers should recognise that marriage and children are not necessarily deterants to full time careers for women. With organised life styles and support from all members of the family, women can succeed in combining careers with the traditional role of women.

The employers should also understand that'pregnancy is not damaging to the brain'. If the society is alien to this idea, then the triple roles of mother, wife and professional cannot be carried out successfully.

A women IAS officer in India states that a woman has to be atleast twice as determined as a man with the same confidence in order to achieve as much as he does.

All of them agree that the basic factor in the success of married women in careers is the cooperation and support of their husbands. Hence the advice is'find understanding men to share your lives - one who would be secure enough in his masculinity to share the responsibility of the home and children and enjoy doing so'

The successful women also feel that the parents have a role to play in their daughters' success. All girls should have the kind of upbringing that gender has nothing to do with what a female could or should do. The parents should help build a strong self image in early childhood; discover and foster the strength of the individuals; encourage hobbies of girls; build a greater sense of caring and respect for the individual person.

Maternal employment has a positive effect on girls. The mother serves as a role model, girls become more autonomous, aspire for careers especially less conventionally feminine careers. The high achieving mother has a high achieving daughter. It has also been found that 24 hour mother is not necessarily a good mother.

Recent research is beginning to show that much of what has hither to been regarded as biologically given or immutable may be quite subject to environmental or external control. There are as many points of difference between men and men and women and women as there are between men and women. For either sex tc use these differences against the other sex is self defeating for both the sexes. The stereotyping of women as the second sex-biologically fragile, emotionally unstable, sensitive, subjective, intuitive and irrational, belies the empirical and experimental data available. Neither are myths such as - men are intellectually superior, men are emotionally more stable than women, men are inherently more assertive than women, men are high in risk taking, creativity, originality, rationality and objectivity are also not proved by experimental research.

The society should demythologize the masculine - feminine, independant - dependant, rational - emotional , competitive - compliant, active - passive dichotomy that has impaired both male and female functioning. To achieve this, both organisational and cultural changes must occur. The cultrual concept that feminine is equivalent to inferior must change. The abilities to cooperate, to express one's emotions and to be intuitive and sensitive can be strengths which are valuable in managerial realms.

In organisations, opportunities for women must be broadened, power must be distributed more widely, women must be hired in large numbers so that proportions are equalized. Hiring by clusters would prevent perpetuation of tokenism.

The 'New Society' should encourage flexibility and individuality for both men and women. The result will be a more effective professional world, a society of happiness, less anxious and more liberated men and women.

Index